THE FOUR SIGNS OF A DYNAMIC CATHOLIC

MATTHEW KELLY

DynamicCatholic.com
Be Bold. Be Catholic.®

THE FOUR SIGNS OF A DYNAMIC CATHOLIC

Published by Beacon Publishing

Printed in the United States of America.[3]

ISBN (Hard Cover): 978-1-937509-26-2
ISBN (Soft Cover): 978-1-937509-66-8

In accordance with the Code Cannon Law,
I hereby grant the Imprimatur ("Permission to Publish")
for *The Four Signs of A Dynamic Catholic.*

Reverend Joseph R. Binzer
Auxiliary Bishop
Archdiocese of Cincinnati
Cincinnati, Ohio, USA
October 24, 2012

The Imprimatur ("Permission to Publish") is a declaration that a book is considered to be free of doctrinal or moral error. It is not implied that those who have granted the Imprimatur agree with the contents, opinions, or statements expressed.

Cover Design: Shawna Powell
Internal Design: Shawna Powell
Author Photo: Peggy McHale Joseph

For more information on this title and other books and CDs
available through the Dynamic Catholic Book Program,
please visit: www.DynamicCatholic.com

The Dynamic Catholic Institute
5081 Olympic Blvd • Erlanger, Kentucky 41018
Phone: 1–859–980–7900
Email: info@DynamicCatholic.com

TABLE OF CONTENTS

ALSO BY MATTHEW KELLY:

Rediscover Catholicism

The Rhythm of Life

The Seven Levels of Intimacy

Perfectly Yourself

Building Better Families

The Book of Courage

A Call to Joy

Mustard Seeds

The Dream Manager

The Shepherd

Why am I Here? (a children's book)

The One Thing

Off Balance

Prologue

ONCE UPON A TIME there was a very successful business owner. His company had faithfully served millions of customers for many, many years. But lately, business had not been so good, and his competitors were just waiting for him to fail. For weeks and months, the man pondered the crisis, but the problems were so complex, and solutions seemed nowhere to be found.

Everyone was wondering what would happen to this great company, so finally the businessman announced that he was hosting a dinner for all of his employees to unveil a plan that would save the company and return it to its former glory. He wanted to convey to them how important each person was to the future success of the organization.

The morning of the dinner, he was sitting in his study at home working on his speech, when his wife came in and asked if he would mind watching their son for a few hours while she ran some errands. He was about to say, "I really need to focus on finishing my speech," but something caught his tongue and he found himself agreeing, reluctantly.

His wife had only been gone about ten minutes when there was a knock on the study door, and there appeared his seven-year-old son. "Dad, I'm bored!" he exclaimed. The father spent the next couple of hours trying to amuse his son while also trying to finish his speech. Finally he realized that if he could not find some way to entertain his child he was never going to get his speech finished in time.

Picking up a magazine, he thumbed through the pages until he came to a large, brightly colored map of the world. He ripped the picture into dozens of pieces, and led his son into the living room. Then, throwing the pieces all over the floor, he announced, "Son, if you can put the map of the world back together I will give you twenty dollars."

The boy immediately began gathering the pieces. He was keen to earn the extra money, as he needed just twenty more dollars to buy a toy he had been saving for since his last birthday. The father returned to his study, thinking he had just bought himself a couple of hours to finish working on his speech, because he knew his seven-year-old son had no idea what the map of the world looked like.

But five minutes later, just as he was settling into his speech, there was another knock on the study door. There stood the young boy holding the completed map of the world.

The father said in amazement, "How did you finish it so quickly?" The boy smiled and said, "You know, Dad, I had no idea what the map of the world looked like, but as I was picking up the pieces, I noticed that on the back there was a picture of a man." The father smiled, and the boy continued. "So, I put a sheet of paper down, and I put the picture of the man together, because I knew what the man looked like. I placed another sheet of paper on top, then holding them tightly I turned them both over." He smiled again and exclaimed, "I figured, if I got the man right, the world would be right."

The man handed his son twenty dollars. "And you've given me my speech for tonight. If you get the man right, you get the world right."

Chapter One

INCREDIBLE POSSIBILITIES

TRANSFORMING PEOPLE one at a time is at the heart of God's plan for the world. It is also essential to developing dynamic marriages, loving families, vibrant parish communities, thriving economies, and extraordinary nations. If you get the man right (or the woman, of course), you get the world right. Every time you become a-better-version-of-yourself, the consequences of your transformation echo through your marriage, family, parish, nation, and beyond to people and places in the future. It is God who does the transforming, but only to the extent that we cooperate. God's grace is constant, never lacking. So our cooperation with God's desire to transform us is essential; it is the variable. Are you willing to let God transform you?

Helping individuals with this transformation from who they are to who they are capable of being is the great work. Is the Catholic Church the best in the world at assisting men and women in becoming all God created them to be? Most people today would say no. We could argue about it, but we shouldn't have to. Should we be unquestionably the best in the world at this? I think so.

For twenty years I have been speaking and writing about the genius of Catholicism. I have done this with the hope that it might help others to catch a glimpse of what Catholicism truly is and how it can transform us, and the world, if we embrace it. I suppose on a very basic level I want others to experience the joy that the Catholic faith has brought to my life.

In my travels I have noticed that some Catholics are more engaged than others, but I never really took the time to explore why. This is a regret I will live with for the rest of my life, because if I had taken the time to really understand the difference between highly engaged Catholics and disengaged Catholics, the work my staff and I have undertaken over these past two decades could have been infinitely more effective. That has all changed now. The ideas within this book have transformed the way I speak, write, and live. But we are getting ahead of ourselves. This is how it all began. . . .

Several years ago I was having dinner with a group of priests in Minnesota before an event. I was the only non-cleric at the table, and some of the priests started talking about different things that were happening in their parishes. One of the priests was very young, and he was lamenting about how few people were actively involved at his parish. My mind was starting to drift toward what I was going to speak about at the event when I heard something that jolted me back into the moment. Sitting at the head of the table like a king was a warm, humorous, and completely down-to-earth priest who must have weighed 350 pounds and been almost eighty years old. Waving a finger down the table, he said to the young priest, "Listen, I have been the pastor of seven parishes over the past forty years, and I can tell you that it doesn't matter where you go, you will discover the same fifty people do everything in a parish."

The comment got my attention. I immediately wondered if it was true. In the following weeks I started making informal phone calls to some pastors I knew. I asked them questions like:

- Who are your most engaged parishioners?
- Why are they so engaged?
- What percentage of registered parishioners are actively involved in the parish?
- What percentage of parishioners give regularly to the parish?

The answers they gave me seemed to anecdotally support the priest's comment, but I wanted data.

There is a concept known as the Pareto Principle. It states, in essence, that roughly 80 percent of effects come from 20 percent of causes. In business this same concept is often referred to as the 80/20 principle. The idea is that 80 percent of your business comes from 20 percent of your customers. For example, while Coca-Cola has literally billions of customers, its largest are companies such as McDonald's, Marriott, and Delta Air Lines, who serve millions of people Coca-Cola products every day. The concept can also be applied to products. Eighty percent of most companies' profits tend to come from 20 percent of their products. For example, consider a Barnes & Noble bookstore. There may be a hundred thousand different titles on the shelves in any given store, but 80 percent of their profits will come from 20 percent of those titles—the books that sell over and over again.

I had always been curious about whether the 80/20 principle would apply to the Church, and the priest's comment had piqued my curiosity. Did the rule hold true in Catholic parishes? The only way to find out for sure would be to obtain some hard data. Over the course of many months I studied a series of parishes from coast to coast, examining two areas in particular: volunteerism and financial contribution. Both are significant signs of engagement. What I found left me speechless.

Did the 80/20 principle hold true in Catholic parishes? No. Not even close. This is what I discovered:

- 6.4 percent of registered parishioners contribute 80 percent of the volunteer hours in a parish
- 6.8 percent of registered parishioners donate 80 percent of financial contributions
- There is an 84 percent overlap between the two groups

Note: Unless otherwise stated, all statistics come from research conducted by The Dynamic Catholic Institute.

I was amazed. Roughly 7 percent of Catholic parishioners are doing almost everything in their faith community and paying almost entirely for the maintenance and mission of the parish. This led me to the seminal question: What is the difference between engaged Catholics and disengaged Catholics? It came as a staggering surprise to discover that there was no significant research available on this question.

The future of the Catholic Church depends upon us finding out what makes this small group of Catholics so engaged. If we cannot identify what drives their engagement, we cannot replicate it.

For the rest of the book I will refer to these highly engaged parishioners as either the 7% or Dynamic Catholics. There is much we can learn from them. It is, however, critical to understand before we go any further that generalizations can provide incredible insight, but they can also be very dangerous if taken too far or out of context. The 7% are by no means perfect, but there is something about them that is worth exploring. Most of them are not spiritual champions, and they would be the first to admit that. They are also often quick to point out that it doesn't take much to be at the top of the heap among Catholics today. The bar is not exactly set very high. But the 7% are the most highly engaged among us. I will refer to their less engaged counterparts as the 93%.

There are almost endless ways to segment both the 7% and the 93%. Not everyone in the 7% is the same. Even among this group, engagement, attitudes, and spiritual habits differ significantly. Needless to say, among the other 93% there are enormous differences. Some in this group come to Mass every Sunday while others are almost completely disengaged. Keep in mind that this group includes everyone from 7.01 percent to 100 percent (more than seventy-one million of the seventy-seven million Catholics in America).

At first I found these results very discouraging, but it turns out this might be the best news the Catholic Church has received in decades. Why is it good news that only 7 percent of American Catholics are highly engaged? Well, think about the tremendous contribution that the Catholic Church makes every day in communities large and small across America and around the world. Every single day we serve Catholics and non-Catholics around the world by feeding more people, housing more people, clothing more people, caring for more sick people, visiting more prisoners, and educating more students than any other institution on the planet. Now remember that all this is less than 7 percent of our capability. That is good news.

If just 7 percent of Catholics are accomplishing more than 80 percent of what we are doing today, imagine what 14 percent could do. Not to mention what 21 percent or 35 percent could accomplish. Our potential is incredible. The Catholic Church is a sleeping giant. We literally have the power to change the world.

If we engaged just another 1 percent of your parishioners over the next year, transforming them into Dynamic Catholics, it would be a game changer. It would result in 11.4 percent more volunteer hours, which would allow you to serve other parishioners and your community that much more effectively. It would also bring about a 11.4 percent increase in revenue, which would allow your parish to invest in powerful and important ministries that would further drive engagement. All this as a result of a shift from 7 percent to 8 percent—just 1 percent more highly engaged Catholics.

Then I started to think, imagine what we could do if we could transform another 7 percent into highly engaged parishioners over the next seven years. One percent each year. It would not mean every person in the parish would be passionately interested and engaged—just 14 percent. And imagine the incredible outreach, service, and spiritual development your parish could deliver.

This is the 1 percent that could change the world. If we can focus on engaging 1 percent more of our parishioners in a really intentional way each year, we can literally change the world. If you have a thousand adults in your parish, that means transforming just ten more into highly engaged members this year.

For months after this discovery, I was constantly thinking about how we could go about increasing the number of Dynamic Catholics in a parish. Then one day the obvious finally occurred to me: We needed to do some more research. We needed to find out what made the 7% different. What do the 7% do, think, and believe that is different from what the 93% do, think, and believe?

The book in your hands holds the answer to that question. There are many things that make the 7% different from the rest of Catholics. But there are four things that the 7% have in common. I have named these four defining attributes and behaviors the four signs of a Dynamic Catholic. These four signs are the life-giving spiritual habits that animate their lives. I am convinced that if we work intentionally to help people develop a vibrant spirituality through these four signs, we will see incredible things happen in their lives and in the life of the Church.

For too long we have been hypnotized by complexity. There is so much to Catholicism. It is so rich and deep. As a result, when we try to share the faith with others they are often quickly overwhelmed. Those who yearn for spiritual renewal in their lives usually don't know where to start. The four signs cut through the complexity and provide a practical and accessible model for engaging Catholics. They provide a simple and understandable starting point. They also provide an enduring model for continually taking Catholics who are already engaged to the next level. Wherever you are in your spiritual journey, whether you are engaged or disengaged, I hope you will find in the four signs a model for renewal.

The Four Signs – an Overview

The things we do repeatedly determine our character and destiny. This is equally true for an athlete, a business leader, a parent, or a Catholic. Life-giving spiritual habits are what set the 7% apart from the rest. When I studied the lives of Dynamic Catholics I discovered many things they did that the other 93 percent of Catholics tended not to do. In fact, I identified 264 behaviors or qualities that were unique to the 7%. I then examined the cause-and-effect relationship between all 264 behaviors, and the overlap that existed among them, to arrive at the four signs of a Dynamic Catholic.

For example, some of the highly engaged Catholics among the 7% pray the rosary every day with great discipline, others attend daily Mass, and some have a big, comfortable chair where they begin each day in prayer and reflection. Each of these finds its place under the first sign: Prayer.

There are some among the 7% who will tell you that going to daily Mass is the very core of their spiritual life. The danger is to think that is the answer for everyone. Daily Mass is fabulous and has transformed many lives, but less than 1 percent of American Catholics go to daily Mass. More important, for most people it is simply not possible. We need solutions that are accessible to all, that inspire people to say, "I can do that!"

There are many ways to live out each of the four signs; I witnessed this among the people interviewed. The four signs are sufficiently focused to produce the intended result and yet sufficiently broad to allow each person to approach them in his or her own way.

Once again, let me point out that the 7% are by no means perfect. In fact, the research discovered many things about them that repel the 93%. The 7% do things that discourage others from becoming more engaged. They can be territorial, excluding others from joining groups or activities. They often speak in a "church language" that the 93% don't understand. They suffer from what I would call spiritual amnesia, meaning that they have forgotten or block out how resistant to God they were at different times in their spiritual journey, or how far from God they have been at times in their lives. This spiritual amnesia robs them of the ability to relate to others who are less engaged. It also often makes them intolerant of less engaged Catholics, thinking that those people should just "get with the program."

Whatever shortcomings the 7% have can be overcome if they

embrace the four signs more completely. The four signs are not only a model to reengage disengaged Catholics but also a model of continuous renewal for even the most highly engaged Catholics.

The Four Signs of a Dynamic Catholic are:

- PRAYER
- STUDY
- GENEROSITY
- EVANGELIZATION

These may not seem like any great discovery at first glance. What I find most fascinating is the way Dynamic Catholics approach each of the four signs. What I find most admirable is the almost unerring consistency with which they apply themselves to the four signs, especially the first and second.

While I have dedicated a chapter to each of the signs, I think it would be helpful to take a quick journey through the entire model as an overview.

THE FIRST SIGN - PRAYER

Dynamic Catholics have a daily commitment to prayer.

God is not a distant force to these people, but rather a personal friend and adviser. They are trying to listen to the voice of God in their lives, and believe doing God's will is the only path that leads to lasting happiness in this changing world (and beyond).

Am I saying the other 93 percent of Catholics don't pray? No. Their prayer tends to be spontaneous but inconsistent. The 7%

have a daily commitment to prayer, a routine. Prayer is a priority for them. They also tend to have a structured way of praying. Many of them pray at the same time every day. For some it means going to Mass in the morning and for others it means sitting down in a big, comfortable chair in a corner of their home or taking a walk, but they tend to abide by a structure.

Some start by simply talking to God about their day. Others begin their prayer by reading from the Bible. Still others have a favorite devotional book that they begin with. When they arrive at the time and place in their day for prayer, they have a plan; it is not left to chance or mood. They have a habit of prayer, which they cling to with great discipline.

This daily habit of prayer is the result of real spiritual work. Different things work for different people. Beginners in prayer struggle because they try one thing and it doesn't work, and they get discouraged. Too many people don't have someone they can turn to and discuss the intricacies of developing a practical and sustainable prayer life. In most cases the 7% have developed their routine of prayer painstakingly through trial and error over the course of decades.

What is important to recognize is that Dynamic Catholics have a time to pray, a place to pray, and a structure to their prayer.

The 93% certainly pray, but it tends to be when the mood strikes them or when some crisis emerges. The 7% pray in this way also, but their spontaneous prayer is deeply rooted in their daily discipline and commitment to a prayer routine.

THE SECOND SIGN - STUDY

Dynamic Catholics are continuous learners.

On average Dynamic Catholics spend fourteen minutes each day learning more about the faith. They see themselves as students of Jesus and his Church, and proactively make an effort to allow his teachings to form them.

Jesus doesn't just want followers. He wants disciples. To be a Christian disciple begins by sitting at the feet of Christ to learn. We all sit at the feet of someone to learn. Whose feet do you sit at? For some it is a talk show host and for others it is a politician; for others still it is a musician, an artist, a pastor, or a business leader. But none of these are a substitute for Jesus. The 7% are keenly interested in learning from Jesus and about Jesus. More than just a historic figure, he is seen as a friend, coach, mentor, and Savior. They believe that Jesus teaches them through the Scriptures, Christian tradition, and the Church.

Highly engaged Catholics read Catholic books, listen to Catholic CDs, watch DVDs about the faith, and tune in to Catholic radio and television programs. They go on retreats more regularly than most Catholics and attend spiritual events and conferences. They are hungry to learn more about the faith. They are continuous learners.

It is also important to note that even though they tend to know much more about the faith than the 93%, they have a position of humility, which is a critical element of the second sign. If they disagree with a Church teaching, they approach the issue in this way: "Why does the Church teach what she teaches?

It is unlikely that I know better than two thousand years of the best Catholic theologians and philosophers. What am I missing?" From this perspective they explore what the Church teaches to further understand God's way, eager to discover the truth.

When the 93% disagree with a Church teaching, they tend to approach it altogether differently. Their attitude tends to be: "The Church is wrong. The Church needs to get with the times. The Church doesn't understand me. I know better than two thousand years of the best Catholic minds." Most striking is that these conclusions are often reached with little more than a surface understanding of what the Church teaches and why.

The second sign is all about continuous learning, the daily discipline of exploring the way of Jesus and the genius of Catholicism.

THE THIRD SIGN - GENEROSITY

Dynamic Catholics are generous.

Dynamic Catholics are filled with a spirit of service and are generous stewards of their time, talent, and treasure.

The 7% are universally described as being generous, not just with money and time, but with their love, appreciation, praise, virtue, and encouragement. They see generosity as the heart of Christianity and the proof that the teachings of Christ have taken root in their lives.

The most fascinating thing that came out of the interviews in relation to the third sign is that Dynamic Catholics believe that it starts with financial generosity. They describe love of money and attachment to the things of this world as a primary impediment to spiritual growth, and see this as something that everyone struggles with regardless of how much or how little we have.

Financially, Dynamic Catholics give several times more to their parish and other nonprofit organizations (as a percentage of their annual income) than their counterparts in the 93 percent.

But it is how comprehensively generosity is woven into their lives and the spontaneity with which they dispense it that was so inspiring to me. They are generous lovers, they are generous parents, they are generous with their colleagues at work, and they are generous with strangers who cross their path. They are generous with their virtue—generous with patience, kindness, and compassion. Generosity is not a religious requirement for the 7%; it's a way of life, a way of bringing the love of God to the world.

THE FOURTH SIGN - EVANGELIZATION

Dynamic Catholics invite others to grow spiritually by sharing the love of God with them.

Having seen how a vibrant spiritual life has transformed them and every aspect of their lives, highly engaged Catholics want others to experience the joy that flows from having a dynamic relationship with God.

Are you an evangelist? This is one of the questions we asked the 7% in the interviews. Less than 1% replied affirmatively. When they replied no, they were asked whom they considered to be an evangelist. The most common answers were evangelical preachers of the past or present. Not even John Paul II got a mention, even though he preached the Gospel to more people than any other person in history. So while evangelization is at the core of our Catholic mission, it is important to note that most Catholics do not resonate with the idea and remain uncomfortable with this concept and practice.

At the same time, Dynamic Catholics regularly do and say things to share a Catholic perspective with the people who cross their paths.

During the interviews, the 7% were asked about the latest Catholic book they had read. They would start talking about the book and we would ask them where that book was now. As often as not they looked confused by the question. We then asked if the book was on their bedside table, on a bookshelf, or somewhere else in the house. They responded, "Oh, no, I gave that book to my friend Suzie at work." They were then asked about the best Catholic CD they had ever heard. "Where is it now?" "I sent that to my son in California," or "I gave that to my friend." And perhaps most telling, the 7% are significantly more likely to invite someone to attend a Catholic event than the 93%.

Though they don't consider themselves to be actively evangelizing, they are constantly trying to help people develop vibrant spiritual lives by discovering the genius and beauty of Catholicism.

In some cases I was able to speak to family and friends of the 7%. In these interviews it became evident that in conversations Dynamic Catholics were much more likely to encourage a perspective that included God and the Church.

It is, however, important to point out that of the four signs, even among the 7%, this is the most underdeveloped. This is where even our best and brightest are the weakest.

Nonetheless, highly engaged Catholics instinctively know that this is an essential part of the Christian life. Sharing the faith (Evangelization) is not something they do; it is a part of who they are. Evangelization is a natural overflow of the first and second signs. In the same way they are generous with their time and money, they generously share their spirituality whenever the opportunity emerges. They yearn to help people find answers to the questions they have about the faith. They want others to experience the joy that comes from having a vibrant relationship with God. But even the most highly engaged Catholics need to become much more intentional and proactive when it comes to the fourth sign.

How Are You Doing?

The four signs can manifest themselves in different ways from one person to the next. But imagine for a moment if everyone in your parish did these four things:

1. Spent ten minutes each day in prayerful conversation with God
2. Read five pages of a great Catholic book each day
3. Gave 1 percent more of their income to support the mission of their parish than they did last year
4. Did one thing each week to share the genius of Catholicism with someone else.

How would your parish be different after one year? How would it be different ten years from now?

Prayer, Study, Generosity, and Evangelization. It is a simple plan, but complex problems demand simple solutions. It is the simplicity that allows widespread adoption and participation.

So, before we move on, how are you doing? Are you a Dynamic Catholic? Give yourself a score between 1 and 10 for each of the four signs over the past year. (Circle your score.) If you wish, go back and reread the descriptions of each of the four signs, one at a time, and then score yourself.

Prayer	1 • 2 • 3 • 4 • 5 • 6 • 7 • 8 • 9 • 10
Study	1 • 2 • 3 • 4 • 5 • 6 • 7 • 8 • 9 • 10
Generosity	1 • 2 • 3 • 4 • 5 • 6 • 7 • 8 • 9 • 10
Evangelization	1 • 2 • 3 • 4 • 5 • 6 • 7 • 8 • 9 • 10

How did you do? Over the course of more than three thousand interviews, the 7% rated themselves at 6.5 on average across all four signs, or 26 out of 40. They rated themselves highest in the first sign (Prayer) with 7.3, lowest in the fourth sign (Evangelization) with 4.9. In the second sign (Study) they rated themselves 6.8 and in the third sign (Generosity) 7. So it is clear that even the 7% realize that they have much room for improvement.

As human beings we have a great psychological need to know we are making progress, and so finding ways to measure progress is critical even in an area like spirituality, which is so difficult to measure.

It is also critical to be mindful that the four signs are interrelated. For example, if you read five pages of a good Catholic book each day (Study), your prayer life would no doubt improve (Prayer), you would be more likely to talk with others about the ideas you are reading about (Evangelization), and the more you know God and his Church the more likely you are to be generous with God and neighbor (Generosity).

In the following chapters we will explore each of the four signs in detail, but I hope this brief overview has been helpful in allowing you to catch a glimpse of the whole model.

Incremental Spirituality

By now you have probably surmised that you are either part of the 7% or you are not. To be honest, I was surprised by how much more disciplined many of the people I interviewed were in each of the four areas than I am at times. The research taught me that I am not as good a Catholic as I thought I was and gave me some very specific areas to grow in.

Whether you consider yourself part of the 7% or not, that was yesterday. Just because you were once in the 7% doesn't mean you will always be. What matters is what you do next. If you are part of the 93% I am so excited for you. Incredible possibilities lay ahead for you—a life more fulfilling than you ever could have imagined. At the Dynamic Catholic Institute we are dedicated to helping you in this journey, and we hope we can give you the tools you need to join the 7%. If you are already part of the 7% we want you to help us attract and engage the 93%.

Wherever you are in the journey, you may be thinking that you just don't have time for anything else. The principle of continuous improvement is about to become your new best friend. All this principle asks you to do is to take one small step, and it can be applied to almost any area of your life. Making small daily investments usually leads to large returns. Here are some examples of what you can apply the principle of continuous improvement to: losing weight, paying off debt, writing a book, improving your marriage, running long distances, increasing the profitability of a business, reading the Bible, and becoming a Dynamic Catholic.

Programs that ask people to make radical and sweeping changes fail the great majority of the time. Examples include diets that require you to cut out all your favorite foods at once, savings plans that insist that you don't buy anything unless it is absolutely necessary, and giving up an addiction cold turkey. Some people succeed in these programs, but the great majority fail. Most of us need a gentler path.

Sometimes Catholicism can seem like one of those very rigid, all-or-nothing plans. We need to find small, simple, nonthreatening ways for people to explore the faith and grow in their spirituality. It is true that God wants to radically transform our lives, and sometimes he calls us to take a great leap. But most of the time he invites us to make small, continuous improvements.

Any suggestion of a single large change to a person's life (or an organization) tends to be met with massive levels of fear, anxiety, and resistance. So the only viable solution is small but consistent steps in a positive direction.

I have read about psychologists who used this method masterfully. In one case a patient who was tremendously overweight was asked to stand on the treadmill for one minute each morning. That's right. Just stand there! Another with the same problem but who was also addicted to television was simply asked to stand up and march in front of the television for one minute each hour. In both cases the patients did not become any healthier over the course of the next week, but their doctor noticed the attitude of each patient had changed.

The suggested change was so small and nonthreatening that they started to think, "I can do that," whereas in the past everything they had been told they needed to do seemed so far out of reach that they shut down and did nothing.

Change in its smallest, least threatening form is usually the most successful.

Now, let's consider the four signs of a Dynamic Catholic. You may be saying to yourself that you have a full, busy, hectic life and that there is no way you can fit the four signs into it. That may be true. But could you spend one minute each day for the next week in focused conversation with God? Perhaps you could set an alarm and try to do it at the same time each day.

One small step! Nobody is so busy that they cannot set aside one minute for a conversation with God each day. It is just one small, seemingly insignificant, nonthreatening step. But if you commit yourself to it and practice it with discipline, you will be amazed how that one minute impacts your day.

After doing that for a week, perhaps the next week you could add reading one page from a Catholic book each day. That's another small step!

The following week you may commit to practicing one intentional act of generosity each day.

The week after that perhaps you decide to pass a Catholic book you have been reading on to someone else.

Then maybe you go to two minutes of prayer, then two pages

of a Catholic book, and so on. Tiny steps, but they will change your life in the most beautiful ways. You will have more joy. You will be more focused. You will have a greater sense of what matters most. Your relationships will improve. Your work will take on new meaning. You will develop the courage and fortitude to endure the inevitable suffering that is a part of each life. And over time you will become heroically patient.

Small changes often seem trivial. They don't scare people or make them overly anxious, because they seem manageable. The reason they seem manageable is because they are. If an enormous transformation can be broken down into small changes, it will meet little resistance.

God wants to transform you and the way you live your life.

In this model of incremental growth we will find the wisdom not only for personal transformation but also to transform our parishes. We all know how busy everyone is. So we need an approach that seems manageable to busy people. We need a plan that leaves people thinking, "Yes, I can do that!"

With our spiritual lives reenergized and our parishes reinvigorated, then, and only then, the Catholic Church will once again become a beacon of hope and inspiration for the world.

One small step!

Would you take one small step if it helped you to make sense of who you are and what you are here for?

Would you take it if . . .

. . . it led to a deep and abiding inner peace?

. . . you believed it would lead to incredible relationships?

. . . you thought it would lead you to a dynamic spiritual life?

. . . it helped you to discover the genius of Catholicism?

. . . you knew it would reinvigorate your parish?

This book is about that next small step. Whatever it is for you, I will be praying that you have the courage to take it. My hope is that I can inspire you to take it, and give you the tools to help others to take a small step each day. At the end of each chapter I hope you can say to yourself, "I can do that!"

Every day God invites me to take one small step toward him. I often resist. Other days I am so enthusiastic and excited I want to run toward him with reckless abandon and make up for so many lost days. But God taps me on the shoulder and says, "Slow down, enjoy the journey—all I ask is for one small step each day."

This book is not about overwhelming you. Wherever you are in your spiritual journey, this book is about taking the next small step toward becoming a Dynamic Catholic. If at any point you feel overwhelmed, you have misunderstood the message.

Certainly I am going to share many ideas and practices with you, but your job is to find the one small step you should be focusing on at the moment and apply it to your life. You may need to come back and read the book several times to really absorb what I am trying to share with you. But each time you read this brief book, focus on the one small step that best suits you at that time in your life. And be sure to take note of the progress you have made since the last time you read this book, or the first time you read this book.

Most people who have accomplished anything worthwhile in their lives will tell you that when they look back it all happened little by little. There is no such thing as overnight success. Life tends to unfold little by little, in incremental steps.

It's time we applied the wisdom of continuous improvement to our spiritual lives. Incremental spirituality allows us to recognize where we are and where we are called to be, and at the same time celebrate our progress.

Intentionality

Henry David Thoreau observed, "In the long run, men only hit what they aim at." My experience with people, teams, and organizations has confirmed this observation over and over. But perhaps most compelling is that when I wander aimlessly into a day at work I tend to get very little accomplished. I may be very busy and get many things done, yet real accomplishment lies not in doing many things but in doing the most important things.

Most of us don't live our lives very intentionally.

What's the first thing most people do when they get to work each morning? Check their e-mail. In fact, most people do it long before they even get to the office. Some check their e-mail when they wake up, even before they get out of bed. But let me ask you, when was the last time you checked your e-mail and thought to yourself, "I'm so glad I checked my e-mail first thing this morning because it really helped me to strategically focus my day"? The opposite is probably true. Checking your e-mail first thing each morning probably prevents you from strategically focusing your day, because you then tend to spend your day responding to e-mail dramas and dilemmas. Meanwhile the real work, the most important work, goes neglected and undone. The most important things are always the easiest to put off, and they tend to require intentionality to accomplish.

About three years ago, I shared with a good friend of mine that I was struggling to get to the most important aspects of my work because I was constantly distracted by meetings, phone calls, e-mails, and other interruptions. The reason I turned to him with this problem was because he works as an executive coach and I figured he had lots of clients with exactly the same dilemma. He suggested that I stop scheduling meetings and conference calls before eleven a.m. each day. This would allow me to use the first and best hours of my day for the most important projects. Then he encouraged me to take twenty minutes each Sunday afternoon to schedule one project to work on each morning for the following week. This simple process has been a game changer for me. Why? At the macro level, it drives intentionality. And at the micro level, fifty percent of most tasks is simply scheduling them. Once you schedule something you are fifty percent of the way to accomplishing it. It is the things we don't schedule that tend never to get done.

Some weeks I don't do it. I don't take those twenty minutes to plan out my week, either because I am lazy, can't be bothered, get distracted, or simply forget. I am always less efficient and effective during those weeks. Without intentionality, one week blends into the next, and little of what matters most gets accomplished.

We tend to stumble through life a day at a time, and look back wondering where a summer, a year, or a decade went. The problem is, you don't stumble into great things, or even worthy things. They have to be sought out with intentionality.

A vibrant spiritual life is one of those great things. People don't just stumble into it. We either actively seek it because we sense that something is missing in our lives, or we are led to it by another person, who recognizes how incredibly our lives would change if we took our spiritual development seriously.

If they felt a call to go to the next level in their spirituality, most Catholics would not know where to start. Many of us are just fumbling along, oblivious to whether or not we have grown spiritually over the past year. This needs to change if we are going to help people thrive. This needs to change if we want our parishes to thrive. As the story from the Prologue suggests, if we get the man or woman right we will get the parish right. It is impossible to separate personal transformation from the transformation of a parish. And transformation doesn't just happen. It requires intentionality.

Intentionality helps us to perform at our best in any area of our lives. The four signs drive this type of intentionality in the spiritual realm.

The Catholic Church in America is in desperate need of renewal, but where do we start? The needs and problems can seem so overwhelming at times, even on a parish level. I believe we should focus our efforts on helping people of all ages to develop vibrant spiritual lives. Everything else, any other good thing that we desire for the Church and for the world, will flow from a dynamic relationship with God. It always has. But renewal will come about only if we approach it with rigorous intentionality. We need to raise the level of intentionality in every realm within the Church.

A Significant Discovery

Imagine if we discovered that all highly engaged Catholics had four things in common. Then imagine if it could be demonstrated that when someone started embracing these four things they were relatively quickly transformed from a disengaged Catholic into a highly engaged Catholic. Would you be interested in knowing what those four things were? And if we had this knowledge, if we knew what these four things were, what would we do with that information? Wouldn't it make sense to intentionally encourage these four things and use them to focus the way we teach and lead?

We now know what those four things are. They are the four signs of a Dynamic Catholic: prayer, study, generosity, and evangelization. It is my hope that they will reinvigorate you, and through you, your parish, so that together we can serve your community and the world in ways that inspire many others to give Catholicism another look.

We have a long way to go in order to live up to God's vision for our lives and his vision for the Church. The people of our times desperately need us to live up to that vision. It is a monumental task. How will we get there? How do we transport whole generations from disappointment and discouragement to hope and engagement? Little by little.

When we become convinced of "I can do that!" our lives begin to flood with hope… and hope is a beautiful thing. It is time for Catholics to be filled again with that hope. The hope that comes from knowing that we have something of immeasurable value to offer to the world. When a group of people becomes full of hope, incredible things begin to happen.

Something wonderful is about to happen!

CHAPTER SUMMARY

INCREDIBLE POSSIBILITIES

- Transforming people one at a time is at the heart of God's plan for the world.
- 6.4 percent of registered parishioners contribute 80 percent of the volunteer hours in a parish, 6.8 percent of registered parishioners donate 80 percent of financial contributions, and there is an 84 percent overlap between the two groups.
- If just 7 percent of Catholics are accomplishing more than 80 percent of what we are doing today, imagine what 14 percent could do. Not to mention what 21 percent or 35 percent could accomplish. Our potential is incredible. We literally have the power to change the world. The Catholic Church is a sleeping giant.
- If a parish engaged just another 1 percent of its parishioners over the next year, transforming them into Dynamic Catholics, it would be a game changer. It would result in 11.4 percent more volunteer hours, which would allow you to serve other parishioners and your community that much more effectively. It would also bring about a 11.4 percent increase in revenue, which would allow your parish to invest in powerful and important ministries that would further drive engagement. All this as a result of a shift from 7 percent to 8 percent—just 1 percent more highly engaged Catholics.
- If we could transform another 7 percent into highly engaged parishioners over the next seven years—1 percent each year—it would not mean every person in the parish would be passionately interested and engaged; it would be just 14 percent. But imagine the incredible outreach, service, and spiritual development your parish could deliver.
- This is the 1 percent that could change the world. If we can focus on engaging 1 percent more of our parishioners in a truly inten-

tional way each year, we can literally change the world. If you have a thousand adults in your parish, that means transforming just ten more into highly engaged members.

- Continuous improvement is a long-term approach that seeks to achieve small, incremental changes. Each change can be so small and simple that, at the time, it seems insignificant, but as you add these changes together over time they become enormous.

- Highly engaged Catholics have four things in common, the four signs of a Dynamic Catholic:

  1. Prayer: Dynamic Catholics have a daily commitment to prayer.

  2. Study: Dynamic Catholics are continuous learners.

  3. Generosity: Dynamic Catholics are generous.

  4. Evangelization: Dynamic Catholics invite others to grow spiritually by sharing the love of God with them.

- This book is not about overwhelming you. Wherever you are in your spiritual journey, this book is about taking the next small step toward becoming a Dynamic Catholic. If at any point you feel overwhelmed, you have misunderstood the message. At the end of each chapter I hope you can say to yourself, "I can do that!"

- You don't stumble into great things, or even worthy things. They have to be sought out with intentionality.

KEY CONCEPTS:

Engagement and Disengagement; The 80/20 Principle; The Four Signs of a Dynamic Catholic; Continuous Improvement; Incremental Spirituality: Intentionality; I Can Do That!; Personal Transformation.

THE FIRST SIGN

PRAYER

Chapter Two

P

ARE YOU SPIRITUALLY HEALTHY?

WHEN I AM SPIRITUALLY HEALTHY, nothing bothers me. This one truth is the fruit of many years of self-observation. When I am spiritually healthy my wife can take forever to get ready, the stock market can drop a thousand points in a day, the flight can be canceled, my favorite team can lose, and my plans can fall apart, but I am able to remain calm and maintain a joyful outlook with a deep inner peace.

I know when I am in a place of spiritual health, and I know when I am not. One of the key indicators of spiritual health seems to be gratitude. When I am spiritually healthy I am grateful. But when I am not, even the smallest things drive me crazy. At those times I tend to be irritable, restless, and discontented. In fact, my attitude toward other drivers on the road between my home and the office is a pretty good barometer of how healthy I am spiritually. If I have a spiritual cold I am just a little bit irritable, a little bit restless, and a little bit discontented. But if I am struggling with a spiritual cancer these indicators go off the charts. Someone around me at work or at home could do the smallest irritating thing and that will be enough to get me all twisted up inside. I may not lose it on the outside, but on the inside I am seething.

When I am not spiritually healthy the only way for me to be happy is for everything to go my way . . . and never does everything go our way. So it becomes an impossible scenario. I cannot remember the last time everything went the way I wanted. Even on our best days things don't always turn out as we hoped. That's life. Learning to be joyful even when things don't go your way is one of the ongoing invitations of the spiritual life.

If I am spiritually healthy I can be happy even when things don't go the way I want them to. The world says that the key to happiness is getting what you want and having things go your way. As a result we spend so much time and energy trying to control people and situations, and in the process we make ourselves sick and miserable—not to mention the suffering this type of behavior inflicts on everyone who crosses our path. If you can be happy only if you get your way, isn't that a horrible way to live?

Anyone can be happy when things go their way. Anyone can be happy when they get what they want. But part of our inheritance as children of God is a way of life that allows us to be joyful even when things don't go our way.

Wouldn't you like to carry within you a joy that cannot be extinguished by anything that happens? Are you willing to work for it? When we are spiritually healthy we experience that joy, and nothing can rob us of it. More than anything else, wherever you are in your life, I hope this book helps you to grow in spiritual health so that you can experience that kind of joy.

How spiritually healthy are you today?

How Do Your Best Days Begin?

Life is a collection of days, and some days are better than others. This may seem obvious, and so we perhaps don't question it. But why are some days better than others?

If you look back over the past couple of months, a few days were probably great, most days were average, some days were not so good, and perhaps there were even a couple of days that were horrible. But what made the difference? Was it something outside your control or something within your influence?

One thing I have discovered as I become more and more conscious of what is happening within me and around me is that if a day doesn't get off to a good start it very rarely finishes as a good day. Once a day gets away from us we tend to go into survival mode. And a day can get away from us in so many ways. In fact, a day will almost certainly go wrong unless we consciously take the time to focus the day first thing each morning.

How do your best days begin? Most people don't know. They have a hunch, but they have simply never thought enough about it or experimented with it. This is the first thing that sets Dynamic Catholics apart. They know how their best days begin, and they use this knowledge to give real direction to their lives at the beginning of each day.

The first sign of a Dynamic Catholic is prayer. More specifically, it is a daily commitment to prayer. Dynamic Catholics universally begin their day with some type of prayer, a spiritual routine that focuses their day. Some settle down in a comfortable chair with their morning coffee. Others go to Mass. Some focus their day by praying the morning offering, and have their main time of prayer at some other time in the day. But all of them begin their day with prayer of some kind, however brief, and on a day when they don't follow their routine they can feel the difference. They feel unfocused, stressed, less conscious of what is happening in and around them, less capable of giving those they care about the love and attention they deserve, and disconnected from God. It is as if they feel disconnected from themselves when they don't start their days in the way that they know works best.

Dynamic Catholics know how their best days begin, and the more mature among them (mature in wisdom, not in age) will do almost anything to defend their morning routine. They would rather get up an hour early than forgo that routine. They know that a day that doesn't start well tends not to end well. It is simply too difficult to shift the momentum of a day.

How do your best days begin? Try beginning your day with prayer, however brief, and observe how it impacts the rest of your day.

A Routine of Prayer

Once upon a time there were three frogs sitting on a leaf of a lily outside the palace of a great king. Two of the frogs decided to jump into the pond. How many frogs are left on the lily leaf? Three. Deciding to do something is not the same as doing it.

The first sign of a Dynamic Catholic is prayer. More specifically it is a daily commitment to prayer. That means that they don't *hope* they get around to praying each day. It is not merely a good intention; it is a priority. Daily prayer has become an ingrained habit for them.

You see, if you ask Catholics, "Do you pray?" they all say yes. But the great majority of Catholics don't have a plan when it comes to prayer. We just pray when the mood strikes us. This type of spontaneous prayer is good and should be a part of all our lives. But it is not enough if we really want to grow in virtue, become a-better-version-of-ourselves, have dynamic relationships, and change the world in the ways God intends us to. The Christian life is simply not sustainable without daily prayer. It is just not likely that you will become (or remain) a patient, compassionate, others-centered person who is focused on what matters most without daily prayer. Highly engaged Catholics have figured this out, and that is one of the reasons why they have a daily commitment to prayer.

Even more specific than a commitment, Dynamic Catholics have a routine of prayer. This was one of the inspiring patterns that showed up over and over again in the research. They have a routine of prayer. What does that mean? Well, they tend to pray at the same time every day. They tend to pray in the same place every day. And they tend to pray in the same way every day.

Too many of us tell ourselves that we will pray when we get around to it. This of course means that on many days we don't get around to it. Over time we are more likely to fall into the habit of not praying every day than we are to fall into the habit of praying every day. The reason is because we tend not to just fall into really good life-changing habits. We tend to fall into bad habits. The good ones need to be sought out intentionally. And prayer is one of them.

What I found even more fascinating is that highly engaged Catholics tend to have what I would call a routine within their routine. While it would be easy to skip over this simple point, that would be a mistake, for this routine within their routine is of crucial importance. It is also probably one of the great accomplishments of their lives, though most of them seem a little oblivious to how much of an achievement it is to establish this routine within the routine.

So, what is the routine within the routine?

One set of questions interviewees were asked surrounded their practice of prayer. They were asked when, where, and how they prayed. The answers to these questions were revealing. But when they were asked to walk us through exactly what they did during their time of prayer we discovered something quite important.

When people would say that they pray in the big leather chair in the corner of their living room each morning at seven o'clock, I would ask them, "What happens when you sit down in that chair?" They would usually respond casually, "I pray," as if that were obvious. But I would then ask them to walk me through exactly what happens and how they pray. This is where they revealed the pattern of a routine within a routine. Here are some of their responses.

"Well, I start with a morning offering and then I talk through my schedule for the day with God."

"I read the Gospel of the day and then I talk to God about how I can live that Gospel more fully."

"I take out my Magnificat and pray the morning prayers."

"I read one chapter of the Bible and then I pick one line that jumps out at me and use that to begin a conversation with God."

"I have this devotional book that I have had for many years and I start by just reading the page for today."

All of this may seem basic, obvious, perhaps even remedial to some, but it isn't. You see, when most people do finally sit down to pray in earnest at some point in their life, it is this routine that they are missing. Most people's first attempt at really praying is a disaster because they don't have this routine. The result is that many people simply stop praying.

Most people when they pray sit down and see what happens, and of course very often nothing happens. So they get frustrated and stop praying. When Dynamic Catholics sit down to pray they don't just see what happens; they have a plan. They have a routine, and a routine within their routine.

Interestingly, the great majority of the 7% were never shown how to develop a routine of prayer and a routine within the routine. They forged their routine by trial and error. They observed themselves and figured out what worked and what didn't work for them through sheer perseverance. Some of them have developed their routine of prayer over decades. Here I think we stumble upon one of the great tragedies of modern Christianity, and perhaps Catholicism in particular. We do an awful lot of talking about prayer, but we spend very little time actually teaching people how to pray. We assume that people know how to pray, but the truth is when most people sit down in the classroom of silence to make an earnest attempt at prayer they haven't got the foggiest idea how to begin.

The first sign of a dynamic Catholic is about helping people establish a routine of prayer. One of the greatest gifts we can give anybody is to help them develop a sustainable prayer life. What I mean by that is that we give them the tools to cultivate a spiritual life and the tools to adapt that spiritual life according to the changing demands and challenges of different stages of their lives. Helping them develop a routine of prayer that works for them is the very first step.

So, how is your prayer life?

There is perhaps nothing more telling about the life of a Christian than the answer to this question. It is one thing to judge the past external behaviors of a person, but it is what is taking place inside a person that speaks most about the future.

Catholics approach prayer across a broad spectrum. There are some who identify themselves as Catholics but refuse to pray or involve God in the decisions of their lives. There are others who pray in a mechanical way, but do so inconsistently and are easily distracted by the happenings of life. There are still others who are very passionate about prayer from time to time, but they are erratic in their practice of prayer. There are those who pray every day and try to involve God in the big decisions of their lives, but cut their time of prayer short as soon as it lacks immediate consolation or becomes difficult. There are those who are committed to the practice of daily prayer, but it is a relatively new endeavor. There are those who have firmly established a habitual routine of prayer through years of faithful practice, and involve God intimately in the daily decisions of their lives. And there are those who yearn for a deeper and deeper relationship with God through prayer and have an almost continuous conversation with him throughout the day.

Where do you fall on the spectrum? I am ashamed to say that I am not as far along as I would like to be. And I am fully aware that I have fewer excuses than most for not being farther along, as I have been given the benefit of knowing much more about the process than most. But the point is, each of us should be working to establish a routine of prayer. Later in the chapter I will give you a simple outline for developing a daily routine of prayer, and a routine within the routine. It is brief and simple, and something that you can begin today.

Nothing will change your life like establishing a solid routine of prayer.

The Classroom of Silence

C. S. Lewis was one of the great Christian voices of the twentieth century. He was best known for his Narnia children's books, but his contribution to Christian thought through his lectures and books on Christian spirituality make him one of the giants of modern Christian times.

During World War II, Lewis wrote a weekly column for *The Guardian*, a London newspaper. The column took the form of a letter each week. The letters were written from the perspective of a senior devil training an apprentice devil. The apprentice devil has been given a task by Lucifer himself, and that task is to win a particular young man's soul away from God and for the devil.

The senior devil's name is Screwtape, the junior "tempter" is Wormwood, and the young man whose soul is being sought is known as "the patient." Screwtape is also Wormwood's uncle. The letters themselves are a combination of humor, spiritual education, inspiration, and uncanny insight into the nature of the predictable ways in which we behave as human beings. These letters were published later as a book titled *The Screwtape Letters.*

When the apprentice devil is first given the assignment, he goes to work immediately, thinking of all sorts of creative ways to tempt the young man he has been assigned. But his uncle Screwtape writes him a stern letter rebuking these efforts. He counsels young Wormwood not to waste his time trying to dream up new ways of tempting man. He further explains that their plan is very simple, that it consists primarily of creating so much noise in the world that man can no longer hear the voice of God in his life.

I am writing in 2012, and so these words were penned by C. S. Lewis more than seventy years ago. When he wrote these words Lewis was prophesying. Prophets are not confined to the Old Testament. Every age has them, and C. S. Lewis was a prophet in his time.

Think of the evolution of noise since he penned these words. At the time television had just been invented, but would not take on great popularity for many years yet. And as the noise has increased in the world, and as we have invited it into our lives, it has become harder and harder for us to hear the voice of God.

It is in the silence that God speaks to us.

This diabolical plan to fill our lives with noise is pure genius for its simplicity. And countering it requires the same simplicity. The more time you spend in silence, the more clearly you will hear the voice of God in your life.

And beyond the silence, it is interesting how some forms of noise lead us closer to God and others lead us far from him. Next time you are listening to the radio, as each song comes and goes, ask yourself: Did that song lead me closer to God or further from God? In the same way, conversations with some people inspire us to be better, while conversations that focus on negativity and gossip have the opposite effect.

In my car I always keep one CD in the player: *Come to the Quiet*, by John Michael Talbot. I love to listen to it on my way to the office in the morning. It is a beautiful collection of morning prayers set to music. It soothes my soul and focuses my mind for the day. It reminds me that God is constantly inviting us to spend some portion of our lives in the quiet, so we can live the rest of our lives to the fullest. The gift of this particular collection of music is that it makes me yearn for more quiet time with God.

I cannot imagine God saying, "Come to the noise," or "Fill your life with noise." It seems God is constantly calling out to us, "Come to the quiet."

Of course, the silence can be excruciating at first. This is why so few people slow down for a dedicated time of prayer each day. Most have tried at some point in their lives, but because they don't know what to do, the quiet becomes too much to handle.

The first attempts at most things are excruciating. A child first trying to walk is a perfect example. Progress is slow, excruciatingly slow at times. They stand and fall, and fall over and over again. Only after weeks and weeks of effort do they take those first steps.

When two people are first dating, silence can be excruciating. Silence on a first date can be the kiss of death for a relationship. But over time as a relationship develops into a great love, two people often learn to enjoy just being with each other in silence. Once their relationship reaches this stage, far from being awkward, the silence can be comforting and powerful. Now they can sit on the couch together and neither has to say anything. They have learned just to be with each other.

A great life of prayer develops in the same way. At first the silence can be excruciating, almost torturous. But over time we learn to tolerate it, and then enjoy it, and before long we find ourselves yearning for more and more of it.

The great mystics such as John of the Cross, Teresa of Avila, Francis of Assisi, Catherine of Siena, and so many others who fill our rich Catholic history came to this place where they could just be with God. Learning just to be with God is truly a thing of beauty.

One of the first requirements of the Christian life is to learn to be comfortable in our own company. If we are not, we will avoid silence and solitude, two of the key ingredients for spiritual growth. But perhaps more important, we will constantly seek the approval of others, because we are afraid to be alone.

I have often noticed in my work with teenagers that the ones who get the faith at that age have stepped away from needing the constant approval of their peer group. They have learned to be comfortable in their own company, and so have been able to resist the push and pull of the pressures placed on them by their peers and the culture.

In some ways, I suppose we are not really ready for life until we have learned to be comfortable alone in the great classroom of silence. For it is out of the silence that clarity emerges. Over the past couple of years I have been presenting a one-day retreat called "Living Every Day with Passion & Purpose." One of the first things I explain to those who attend is that we tend to look at people who live with great passion and purpose and think to ourselves that we would like that for ourselves. What most people fail to realize is that passion and purpose are the by-products of something else: personal clarity. Those who live with passion and purpose have more personal clarity than most people. They have a greater sense of who they are and what they are here for. They know what matters most, and this empowers them to focus and prioritize their days. Where do they get this personal clarity? In the classroom of silence.

Clarity emerges from silence. You know this instinctively. If you are taking a road trip with a car full of people and you get lost, what does the driver ask everyone to do? Turn off the radio and be quiet. Why? When you need laser clarity you want silence. Lots of people who work listening to music turn the music off when they really need to concentrate on something. Why? Clarity emerges from silence. And people who live with high levels of passion and purpose are not afraid of spending some time alone in silence to work out who they are, what they are here for, and what matters most.

In this way it seems that God is always saying to me, "Come to the quiet." The world is noisy and distracting. It is in the silence that we find God and our true self.

In the Scriptures we read again and again about Jesus going away to a quiet place. When I am sitting in Mass on Sunday and I hear one of the readings that talk about Jesus going away to a quiet place, I yearn for that myself. I am reminded of how much I need to step back from the hustle and bustle of life for a few minutes each day into a quiet place. At the same time, I know how difficult it is to actually do it. For twenty years I have been encouraging people to carve out ten minutes a day to spend in silent prayer and reflection. And yet, still, on most days I have to force myself to do it. Sure, there are some days when I would rather spend those few minutes in prayer than do anything else in the world. But I must be honest with you, those days are few. Even though I know all the benefits and privileges that come from prayer, even though I know prayer puts me at my best, even though I know these few minutes maintain my spiritual health, I still have to drag myself to prayer on many days.

If it is important to spend time in the quiet, it is also important to have quiet places to go to. In the Scriptures, when we read about Jesus going off to a quiet place, it does not say he went off *looking for* a quiet place. It says he went off to a quiet place. This presupposes that he knew where he was going. Perhaps while he was walking into the village earlier that day he noticed a place and thought to himself that it would be a perfect spot for some quiet time.

In the same way, we all need our quiet places, places we can go to when we need to step back from the world. We need quiet places set apart from the hustle and bustle of our very noisy and busy modern lives. Again, this requires some intentionality. The world draws us toward noisy places, so quiet places can be harder and harder to find. They are not going to just mystically appear at that moment in the day when we need them most. We need to plan.

I have everyday quiet places and once-a-year quiet places, and I think we need both. My everyday quiet places include a number of churches and chapels close to my home, the rocking chair out on the back porch, the leather chair in my study, and the beach. Where is your favorite quiet place? When were you last there? Should you be thinking about going there more often? How would your life be different if you did?

The quiet is critical to our spiritual development because it is in the silence that God speaks to us. We pray for many reasons, and one of those reasons is to seek the will of God for our lives. Without the silence it becomes almost impossible to discern God's will.

One of the great struggles of the Christian life is surrendering our will so that we can embrace the will of God. In my conversations with Dynamic Catholics it became very clear, very quickly, that they believe the only way to secure any lasting happiness in this life (and the next) is by seeking the will of God and trying to fulfill it to the best of their ability. Part of their decision-making process, whether the decision is large or small, is to consider what God's desire is in any given situation. When was the last time you set aside what you wanted and surrendered to what you felt God wanted instead?

God desires nothing but good things for us. So when we speak of following the will of God, we are entering into a process of discernment to discover the good that God desires for us. Too often we resist God's will. We can spend all of our energy fighting him for things we don't really need, instead of surrendering to his perfect plan for our lives.

God, what do you think I should do? I call this the big question. It has been my experience that it is the only question that leads to peace and fulfillment.

When was the last time you consciously sat down and explored God's will for a particular situation? In this way, highly engaged Catholics are committed to listening to the voice of God in their lives. At the same time, they will be the first to admit that they don't always get it right, that it is almost never totally clear, and that at times they know exactly what God is calling them to do but ignore his will. And yet, over and over they learn that it is openness to God's voice and God's will that most brings them peace in the decisions they make.

Develop the habit of spending a few minutes each day in silence and you will have more clarity about every aspect of your life and peace deep in your soul. Clarity emerges from silence, and passion and purpose are the fruits of clarity. If we can raise up a new generation of Catholics who live with passion and purpose, we will once again capture the attention of our age for Christ and the genius of Catholicism.

The Routine within the Routine

When I first set about planning this chapter I noticed myself falling into the obvious trap. It is a trap we fall into all the time at work, at home, and at church. I was tempted to speak to you about many, many different forms of prayer: ancient and modern, personal and communal, etc. There are thousands of different methods and forms of prayer. But one of the important lessons the four signs have taught me is the absolute need for focus and simplicity. If we are to succeed at implementing anything with ourselves (or with large groups of people), simplicity and focus are essential. Every additional option creates a layer of complexity, and every layer of complexity reduces effective implementation.

So I turned my mind toward this question: If you could get every Catholic to pray in the same way for ten minutes each day, how would you encourage them to spend that ten minutes?

The Prayer Process is that one way.

If you really want to markedly improve your life and are serious about growing spiritually, this is the one prayer that I recommend to you. Commit yourself to this practice for ten minutes daily and you will advance spiritually like never before.

The prayer I am referring to is an adaptation of the daily examination of conscience. The idea of examining our conscience before going to Confession is a long-standing part of our Catholic tradition. But too often the concept carries with it a negative connotation. But in reality, examining ourselves can and should be an incredibly positive experience. Far from being about self-deprecation and self-loathing, it is about peace and liberty, awareness and spiritual growth.

Paul advised the early Christians, "Let a man examine himself." (1 Corinthians 11:28) This was particularly in reference to some type of examination before receiving the Eucharist. The hermit Saint Anthony examined his conscience every night before retiring. Over time this became a daily practice in many monasteries, and most founders of religious orders include a daily examination of conscience as a requirement for all members.

Interestingly, I read recently that in the prayer life of priests and religious the deterioration of one's spiritual life begins with skipping the daily examination of conscience. They may still attend Mass and pray the Divine Office, go to holy hour and pray the rosary, but once the daily examination is set aside real spiritual growth ceases, and in time spiritual decay begins.

Bernard of Clairvaux wrote, "As a searching investigator of the integrity of your own conduct, submit your life to a daily examination. Consider carefully what progress you have made or what ground you have lost. Strive to know yourself. Place all your faults before your eyes. Come face to face with yourself, as though you were another person."

But most known for furthering the use and popularity of the daily examination is Saint Ignatius of Loyola. Ignatius began the first week of his famous *Spiritual Exercises* encouraging participants to engage in the daily practice of examining one's soul and life. He believed that the daily examination, which is often referred to as the *Examen*, was the most important of the spiritual exercises.

Today the practice has fallen into disuse, like so many of the best practices of our faith. Marred by a negative overtone and caught in an age when people want to think only about their strengths, the practice of taking an honest look at ourselves in order to improve has fallen by the wayside.

One of the real treasures that this practice delivers is an increased awareness of who we are and what is happening in us and around us. This awareness heightens our ability to experience life. That's right, it actually increases our capacity for life. And in this way, what we are talking about is an examination of consciousness as much as an examination of conscience. This ancient spiritual practice constantly poses the question: How conscious are you? It challenges us to become aware of everything that is happening within us and around us, so that we can live at the height of consciousness.

Very often we wander through a day, a week, a month, or even a year with very little consciousness, almost oblivious to what is really happening inside us and around us. The daily examination of conscience challenges that by liberating us from living unconsciously.

It would seem to me that people are becoming less and less aware of themselves. Many of the things we do and say scream: I am completely unaware of how the way I speak and act affects the people around me!

I promise if you apply yourself to this practice of prayer it will change your life, and it will not take one hundred years for you to realize it. Commit yourself to practicing the Prayer Process for ten minutes each day for thirty days, and by the end of the thirty days I am confident you will be convinced.

The Prayer Process, an adaptation of the examination, provides a consistent format to guide you in your daily prayer. The first barrier to entry for most people who feel drawn to prayer is that they simply don't know how to pray. They have never been taught to pray. It is amazing how little time we as a Church spend teaching people to pray. The Prayer Process overcomes the first barrier to entry by providing people with a format and a method. It provides the routine within the routine that Dynamic Catholics have spent decades developing through the painstaking process of trial and error.

In developing the Prayer Process I have used it with several focus groups, all of whom reported significant spiritual growth when they faithfully practiced the method daily.

This prayer is a game changer for you spiritually, and a game changer for every aspect of your life. If every Catholic in America prayed in this way for a few minutes each day the Church would be on the fast track to renewal. If everyone in your parish began to pray using this process your parish would explode with enthusiasm and engagement.

But don't take my word for it. Whether you start with one minute a day or go straight to the full ten minutes, use the Prayer Process every day for thirty days. If you do, I think you will very quickly be convinced of its power.

Here is the process in its simplest form.

The Prayer Process

1. Gratitude: Begin by thanking God in a personal dialogue for whatever you are most grateful for today.

2. Awareness: Revisit the times in the past twenty-four hours when you were and were not the-best-version-of-yourself. Talk to God about these situations and what you learned from them.

3. Significant Moments: Identify something you experienced today and explore what God might be trying to say to you through that event (or person).

4. Peace: Ask God to forgive you for any wrong you have committed (against yourself, another person, or him) and to fill you with a deep and abiding peace.

5. Freedom: Speak with God about how he is inviting you to change your life, so that you can experience the freedom to be the-best-version-of-yourself.

6. Others: Lift up to God anyone you feel called to pray for today, asking God to bless and guide them.

7. Finish by praying the Our Father.

• • • • • • •

Each of the first six steps in the process should stimulate a conversation with God. It is easy to fall into the trap of merely thinking about these things. When you find yourself doing that, return to actually speaking with God about whatever it is you are thinking. The goal is to develop the ability to have intimate conversations with God during this time set aside for prayer. The more deeply rooted we become in this daily habit of prayer, the more those conversations with God will spill over into the moments of our daily lives.

If you are just beginning, you may want to start with just one minute of conversation with God each day, adding a minute each week until you reach ten. If that is the case, don't try to race through all seven aspects of the prayer process. Just use the first step, Gratitude. Spend your minute speaking to God about everyone and everything you are grateful for, and then close with an Our Father. As you expand your time of prayer over the coming weeks, adding minutes, I suggest you add one step at a time of the process to your daily prayer. The key is to get the conversation started.

But whether you start with one minute a day or ten minutes a day, I hope this chapter has left you thinking, "I can do that!" Nothing will change your life more meaningfully than developing a vibrant and sustainable prayer life.

The Prayer Process is infinitely expandable and contractible. If you went away on retreat you could spend hours praying your way through the process, looking not just at the past twenty-four hours, but at the past year—or even your whole lifetime. For example, the first step in the process surrounds gratitude. Imagine how long you could speak to God about everything that has ever happened in your life that you are grateful for. On the other hand, perhaps on a particular day you don't get to pray at your regular time and then the day gets away from you. Rather than going to bed without doing the Prayer Process because you don't have the will or the energy to pray for ten minutes, shorten the experience. Take just a minute, still go through each of the seven steps, but just speak to God briefly about one thing in each step.

The goal of the Prayer Process is to trigger a regular and meaningful conversation with God.

Prayerlessness: The Curse of Our Age

Prayerlessness is one of the great torments of modern times. For decades the time we spend in focused prayer has been diminishing as our lives have become busier and busier. We have fallen into the tyranny of the urgent, which demands that we rush from one urgent thing to the next. The problem with this is that the most important things are hardly ever urgent. This can leave us always doing urgent things but never doing important things. It is these most important things that we are never getting around to in this cycle. Prayer is one of those important things, and among the highest priority. Prayer helps us to identify what matters most and strengthens our hearts and minds to give priority to those things in our daily lives. What could be more important than prayer?

Prayerlessness also distorts the human person. Without prayer, over time we forget the attitudes and qualities that make us uniquely human (compassion, generosity, humility, fortitude) and we become more and more like mere animals.

Prayer leads us to catch a glimpse of the-best-version-of-ourselves, and helps us to develop the virtue necessary to celebrate our best selves. If you watch your evening news tonight you will discover that the world desperately needs men and women of prayer and virtue. People in your neighborhood need your prayers, your parish needs your prayers, and your colleagues at work need your prayers. And it is painfully obvious at times that the Catholic Church is in desperate need of prayer.

Over the years I have encountered many great families in my travels. A number of years ago I started trying to work out what made these families so steadfast and full of life. Tolstoy begins the epic novel *Anna Karenina* with these lines: "Happy families are all alike; every unhappy family is unhappy in its own way." What I have discovered is that all the great families I have encountered have a giant of prayer. These prayerful giants pray constantly for their families, surrounding them with God's protection. Somewhere in their not-too-distant past is a person who was a prayerful giant. A prayerful giant is a person who covers their family with prayer, anchoring the family in God's grace. Sometimes it is the grandmother or grandfather, the mother or father, an uncle or aunt, and from time to time you have to go back two or three generations, sometimes more. But you always find a prayerful giant in their family tree. Every family needs a cornerstone of prayer to pray for the family, now and in the future.

I suppose if a family gets far enough down the road from that prayerful giant without raising up another, its members begin to lose their way. Does it take a generation or two, or three or four? I don't know. I suppose it depends on many variables. But in each generation, each family needs at least one of these men and women of faithful prayer to guide and protect it.

It has always amazed me that when I am writing a book, a number of people and experiences cross my path to fill in the gaps. It is almost as if God were whispering in my ear. As I was working on a draft of this chapter I had one of those moments. I was at dinner in Los Angeles and I asked my hosts some questions about themselves and their lives. What I heard was the story of a prayerful giant.

My curiosity was piqued when I discovered that my hosts have six children and twenty-two grandchildren and they are all practicing Catholics. Wherever I go, I encounter parents and grandparents who are heartbroken because their children or grandchildren have left the Church. So I wondered who were the prayerful giants in the past and the present of this family. My hosts were Kathleen and Allen Lund. This is Kathleen's father's story.

On the afternoon of January 24, 1945, American soldier Eddy Baranski was executed at the Nazi concentration camp in Mauthausen after being brutally tortured for days. He was a son, a husband, and a father. His father never spoke his son's name again for the rest of his life. His mother prayed for her boy every day for as long as she lived. His young wife, Madeline, had a vision of him smiling at her, at what she would later learn was the very moment of his death. And his daughter, Kathleen, who was just two years old when her daddy went off to fight Hitler, spent the next fifty years fatherless, unable to remember his voice, his touch, or his smell.

Fifty years later Kathleen's daughter participated in a study abroad program in Austria, and while visiting her Kathleen decided to go to Mauthausen. There she stood in the basement where her father had been tortured and shot in the head. She stood there as if waiting for something—some feeling, some message—but there was nothing.

Returning home, Kathleen began inquiring more about her father. She spoke with relatives, wrote to the National Archives, to museums in Europe, and to the United States Army, and slowly, the story of a father she had never known began to emerge.

In 1945 Werner Muller, a German citizen, dictated an extraordinary document to an Austrian lieutenant. The multilingual Werner had worked as an interpreter under Heinrich Himmler. In October 1944 Muller was ordered to Mauthausen, where his job was to translate the interrogations of Allied prisoners. He described the next three months as a living hell. Muller remembered one prisoner above all: Eddy Baranski.

He described Baranski praying as a group of Nazi officers tortured him. The commandant asked the interpreter what he was saying, and when Muller revealed that he was praying the officers all burst into laughter. They then offered him a drink by placing water on a table, but the torture had left him incapable of raising his arms or hands, and they would not raise the water to his mouth. Muller described this as the most miserable afternoon of his life.

Little by little, the story of the father she had lost so early in life was coming together for Kathleen. A couple of years later she visited Piest, Slovakia, where her father had been captured, and the house where he was living at the time of his arrest. There she met Maria Lakotova, who wept when she remembered Eddy Baranski, who used to sing lullabies to her at night when she was a young child in that house.

"Your father would hold me. I would sit on his knees and he would sing to me." Maria told Kathleen. "But I know he was not singing to me; he was singing to you, his little girl so far away."

Kathleen never knew it, but her father was singing to her—and praying for her. Eddy Baranski was a giant of prayer. Every family needs at least one. Today Allen and Kathleen are continuing the legacy by praying for their children and grandchildren each day.

Parishes are like large families in many ways. Every parish needs some prayerful giants to surround the parish with prayer. Our world is racing more and more toward an individualistic world, and the parish is one of the casualties of this rampant focus on self. Many people come to Mass on Sunday but never participate beyond that. They don't engage the community and the community doesn't engage them. Furthermore, they can often come and go on a Sunday without speaking to anybody else except during the sign of peace. It is, for these people, a wholly personal experience devoid of communal meaning. To explore how far-reaching this attitude might be, ask yourself: What percentage of your parishioners have prayed for the parish outside of the Mass in the past thirty days? This is one of the highest indicators of engagement. We have not conducted research on this question yet, but you can be sure it is a very, very small percentage. Like families, parishes need giants of prayer to guide and protect them.

Have you ever known a really prayerful person? What did you notice about that person? Your family, your parish, the Church, and the world need you to become a giant of prayer.

Personal prayer is essential to the Christian life, but so is communal prayer. I would be remiss if I did not mention the enormous importance the 7% place on the role of grace in their lives, and the Eucharist is their primary source of that grace. They have tried to do life on their own, and have come to the conclusion that they would rather try to do life with God. Dynamic Catholics recognize that they are imperfect and struggling in various areas of their lives. They recognize that they cannot get to the next level in their spiritual life or in their relationships on their own. They know they need God and his grace, and they need community. They come to Mass seeking this grace and community. For this reason and others, the Mass is central to their lives. Many of them identify it as the crown jewel of the spiritual life.

Personal prayer is a deepening of your relationship with God, discovering who God is calling you to be for him and for others. The liturgical prayer of Sunday Mass is the prayer of the whole Church gathered as a public proclamation of who we are as Catholics. What you bring to Mass on Sunday is your prayer life, and the deeper it is, the more deeply you can enter into the public expression of the faith of the Church. The Mass is not simply about you; it is the whole Church gathered as a sign of hope to the world. A community at prayer is a beautiful thing.

The first sign of a Dynamic Catholic is prayer. Dynamic Catholics are first and foremost men and women of prayer, just as the saints were. Is it enough for us just to pray? No. We have been given the mission to transform the world. But the best action springs forth from a vibrant prayer life. Our efforts to transform society into a more loving and just experience for all must be deeply rooted in our Christianity, and thus deeply rooted in prayer. Otherwise our Christian social efforts can become disconnected from our Christianity, and this quickly diminishes into just another form of social work. Don't get me wrong—social work is good, but we are called to more than that.

I encourage you to begin (or renew) your commitment to a life of prayer today. Use the Prayer Process to guide you. If you do, I am confident that you will find it is a faithful guide that will lead you deep into a lifelong friendship with God. What are you going to do in this life that is more fulfilling than developing a friendship with God?

One of the great moments in the life of a Christian comes when we realize, once and for all, that a life with prayer is better than a life without prayer.

CHAPTER SUMMARY

PRAYER

- When we are spiritually healthy, nothing bothers us.
- The most dominant quality among Dynamic Catholics is a daily routine of prayer.
- A daily routine refers to a specific time and place set aside for prayer. Dynamic Catholics make this time a priority each day.
- More than just a time and a place to pray, Dynamic Catholics have a routine within their routine. When they sit down to pray each day, they don't just see what happens; they have a routine within the routine. They tend to begin their time of prayer in very specific ways: by reading the Bible, praying the morning prayers of the Church, reading from a favorite spiritual book, etc.
- Dynamic Catholics universally begin their day with some type of prayer, even if the main time they set aside for prayer is later in the day.
- God speaks to us in the silence. Spending time in the classroom of silence is indispensable in our quest for spiritual growth.
- The Prayer Process is a seven-step tool designed to help us develop a routine of prayer, and the routine within the routine.
- Prayerlessness is one of the great torments of modern times.
- Every family needs a prayerful giant.
- At some point Dynamic Catholics have become convinced that a life with prayer is better than a life without prayer.
- Most Catholics have never been taught how to develop a daily routine of prayer.

- Dynamic Catholics see a connection between the joy and fulfillment in their lives and their efforts to walk with God and grow spiritually.

- The Prayer Process

    1. Gratitude: Begin by thanking God in a personal dialogue for whatever you are most grateful for today.

    2. Awareness: Revisit the times in the past twenty-four hours when you were and were not the-best-version-of-yourself. Talk to God about these situations and what you learned from them.

    3. Significant Moments: Identify something you experienced today and explore what God might be trying to say to you through that event (or person).

    4. Peace: Ask God to forgive you for any wrong you have committed (against yourself, another person, or him) and to fill you with a deep and abiding peace.

    5. Freedom: Speak with God about how he is inviting you to change your life, so that you can experience the freedom to be the-best-version-of-yourself.

    6. Others: Lift up to God anyone you feel called to pray for today, asking God to bless and guide them.

    7. Finish by praying the Our Father.

- The first sign of a Dynamic Catholic is Prayer.

KEY CONCEPTS:

Spiritual Health; Daily Routine of Prayer; Routine Within the Routine; the Classroom of Silence; the Prayer Process; Giants of Prayer.

THE SECOND SIGN

STUDY

Chapter Three

THE GENIUS OF CATHOLICISM

FROM TIME TO TIME, we all need to step back from life and take another look at who we are, where we are, and what we are doing. If we don't do this regularly, we tend to get caught up in our own little world—and that is a dangerous place, because it distorts the way we see the world at large, and the way we see the world determines the way we live our lives. How do you see the world? What's your worldview?

Today there are seven billion people on the planet, but imagine for a moment that the whole world is a village of one hundred people. If we reduced the world's population to one hundred people, proportionally, this is how the world would look: Fifty-seven of those one hundred people would come from Asia, twenty-one from Europe, nine from Africa, eight from North America, and five from South America. Fifty-one would be women and forty-nine would be men. Six of those one hundred people would own or control more than 50 percent of the world's wealth, and five of these six people would be U.S. citizens. One of those one hundred people would have just been born, one would be just about to die, and only seven of those one hundred people would have been to college. Thirty-three would be Christian and sixty-seven would be non-Christian. Eighty would be living in substandard housing. Thirty-one would be unable to read and write. Twenty-four would have no electricity. Seventy-one would not have access to the Internet. Thirty-nine of the one hundred people in the village would live on less than two dollars a day. One-third of the world's population is dying from lack of bread, one-third of the world's population is dying from lack of justice, and one-third of the world's population is dying from overeating. How do you see the world?

A simple sketch like this challenges the way we see the world, and draws us out of our own little world. Our worldview constantly needs challenging. Your worldview is made up of a million thoughts, ideas, beliefs, and prejudices. It is unique to you, and largely formed by your past experiences and education. For these reasons your worldview has blind spots and is imperfect. My worldview is distorted and imperfect in the same way. These blind spots and distortions cause us all sorts of problems in life, especially in relationships. This is why God is constantly challenging our worldview.

Jesus challenged the worldview of every person he encountered: Zacchaeus, the woman at the well, the woman caught in adultery and her accusers, Pontius Pilate, Herod, the chief priests and scribes, the rich young man, Lazarus, the disciples . . . Jesus came, among other things, to bring us to a new worldview.

For many years I have been speaking about the genius of Catholicism, a comprehensive and coherent worldview that starts with a vision for the human person.

Have you ever encountered a single idea that turned your life upside down? I had an experience like this when I was about fifteen years old. I was born into a Catholic family and baptized as a child, went to Catholic grade school and high school, went to Mass on Sundays and prayed before meals, but I never really got it. It wasn't until I encountered one idea that turned my life inside out, but right side up, that Catholicism clicked for me. The idea that caused it all to fall into place for me was God's vision for the human person passed on by the Church.

It is a very simple idea. God calls you to holiness, and everything that happens in your life, every triumph, trial, and tragedy, is an opportunity to grow in holiness. When you work hard and pay attention to the details of your work, you grow in virtue and character—and holiness. When you are patient with your little sister or a customer who drives you crazy, you become more perfectly who God created you to be—and you grow in holiness. When you develop a daily routine of prayer and practice it persistently, you develop a closer relationship with God—and you grow in holiness. Every moment has meaning. Every moment of every day presents you with an opportunity to grow in holiness by loving God, loving your neighbor, and becoming more perfectly the unique and wonderful person God created you to be. This was the idea that captured my attention and led me to truly embrace Catholicism for myself, because it revealed the true meaning and purpose of life. And it happened in a way that allowed me to see the connection between the individual events of my daily life and what God was inviting me to through the

Church. This is a vital connection that the Church is failing to make for too many people. It is crucial that we make the connection between the ordinary activities of life and the dream God has for each person if we want to genuinely engage people. At that early time in my life, I saw that everything I did mattered. In every moment I was either celebrating or betraying my best self.

When I first started speaking and writing I noticed that the idea of being called in a personal way to live holy lives was not resonating with people in the way that I had hoped it would. It was from this experience that the phrase "the-best-version-of-yourself" emerged. I would speak about the universal call to holiness and notice the eyes of my audience glazing over. For whatever reason, the language was not connecting with them. The quest for holiness and the quest to become the-best-version-of-yourself are the same concept, but the language seemed more accessible to people. When I explained to them that God has an incredible dream for each and every one us—God wants you to become the-best-version-of-yourself—their eyes began to light up. I knew the message was meeting them where they were and resonating with them.

The genius of Catholicism is that everything makes sense in relation to this one idea. Whether you want to use the phrase "growing in holiness" or "becoming a-better-version-of-yourself" is entirely up to you. For me they are the same. You cannot become the-best-version-of-yourself (or even a-better-version-of-yourself) without growing in holiness.

What makes a good friend? Someone who helps you become the-best-version-of-yourself. What makes a good meal? Food that helps you become the-best-version-of-yourself. What makes good books, movies, and music? Those that inspire you to become the-best-version-of-yourself. What is the meaning and purpose of marriage? Husband and wife coming together, challenging and encouraging each other to become the-best-versions-of-themselves, and then raising children and teaching them to celebrate the-best-version-of-themselves. What is the meaning of work? Is it making money? No. The primary value of work is that when we work hard we become a-better-version-of-ourselves.

I have often been challenged by people saying that striving to become the-best-version-of-yourself seems like a very selfish aim. Not so. In fact, nothing could be further from the truth. Every time I become a-better-version-of-myself, in even the smallest way, I become a better husband, father, son, brother, manager, neighbor, parishioner, citizen, and Catholic. If you extend the idea one step further you discover that every time you become a-better-version-of-yourself, your parish becomes a better parish, the company you work for becomes a better organization, and your country becomes a better nation. As we discovered in the Prologue, personal transformation is at the heart of renewing the world in the way God intends. The best thing you can do for anyone else is to grow in holiness (become a-better-version-of-yourself).

Everything makes sense in relation to this single idea. Life is about saying yes to the things that help you to grow in holiness (become the-best-version-of-yourself) and no to the things that don't. Life is about searching each moment and discovering how that moment is inviting you to become the-best-version-of-yourself. It's disarmingly simple, but not easy. Of course, we make life a lot more complicated for ourselves by not realizing that this is what it is really all about. But you could spend a whole lifetime just unpacking this one idea. Here is a simple example. Tomorrow, in each moment of the day, ask yourself: What can I do right now that will help me become the-best-version-of-myself? For just one day, do only those things that help you become a-better-version-of-yourself.

This is the incredible vision for the human person that the Church has announced with consistency since Christ walked the earth. At times the Church struggles to announce it in a way that meets people where they are and inspires them to leave the ways of world behind and follow Christ more closely. Nonetheless, the Church has been a faithful guardian of this vision.

The reason this vision for the human person is so important is because our view on everything else flows from this primary vision. An authentic Catholic vision for education emerges from our vision for the human person, as does a Catholic vision for health care, family, marriage, health and well-being, entertainment, end-of-life issues, money, finances and the proper use of resources, social justice, and anything else that you might experience in this life. When our view on anything is divorced from this primary vision for the human person, our distortion of reality begins. If you start a little off course, it is amazing how lost you can become. If a plane flying from London to New York changes its direction just five degrees south, it will end up in Venezuela.

It is not possible to carry out the mission God has given us as Catholics and at the same time do things that cause people to become less than who God desires them to be. If we are not helping people to grow in holiness we have strayed from the primary vision God has for all people (and the vision he has for his Church).

This is also what sets the Catholic vision apart from the present culture. Consider this one question: What is the present culture's vision for the human person? When you ask the question, the silence is deafening. Today's culture doesn't have a vision for the human person. The culture doesn't have a vision for you. It certainly does not have your best interests at heart. What, then, is the culture driven by? Consumption. The goal of today's culture is consumption. When was the last time you saw someone being interviewed just because he was a good person with an unusual degree of wisdom, but he had nothing to sell? It is very rare. Almost every person being interviewed is selling something. And if the culture does not have a vision for the human person, then it certainly does not have a vision for your marriage, or your family. In fact, the culture would prefer that every family be broken. Why? A broken family needs two of everything, and that drives consumption.

Too many people have bought into the secular culture because of the sheer momentum it can place on our lives, unless we are actively thinking about life. Too few realize that while it is true we still live in a consumer society, we are no longer the consumers—we are being consumed. It is time for us to start thinking about where our lives are leading and to where God is calling us.

We need to start thinking about our lives on a deeper level. It is time for us to renew our desire for truth and wisdom, and develop a daily habit of study.

The ways of the world lead to confusion and chaos; God's way leads to clarity and order. Is your life in order? The ways of the world lead to meaninglessness and despair; God's way leads to meaningful living and joy. The world or God? Chaos or order? It is a choice we all have to make.

A World Without Truth

There is genius in Catholicism, but the world doesn't see it that way. Today's secular culture rejects the Catholic worldview and instead chooses relativism as its champion. Relativism is the most insidious philosophy of our age. It steals away all meaning from life, and in doing so robs us of the joy God wants us to live with. Joy is simply not possible without meaning. Pope Benedict XVI said this about it: "Relativism, which considers all opinions true even if they are contradictory, is the greatest problem of our time." Think about that for a moment. Consider all the problems in the world today, and yet he says relativism is the greatest of all of them.

So, what is relativism? It is the theory that there are no absolute truths, but rather all truth is relative. That is, something that is true for you may not necessarily be true for me. This leads to an environment in which every person can do whatever he or she wants to do. This philosophy is full of contradictions, because the idea that nothing is absolute is itself an absolute statement. Relativism is usually confined to the area of morals and ethics. In other areas relativists will concede that everything scientifically verifiable is true, but that anything that cannot be scientifically verified is not. The problem is, you cannot scientifically verify this statement. Relativism holds that it is true for everybody that nothing is true for everybody. This, of course, is a self-contradictory proposition.

The problem is most of us don't think enough about life, and little bits of errant philosophies like relativism can stick to us easily enough as we make our way through this world. They are presented under the guise of being open-minded or tolerant. But it is good to be close-minded about certain things—even before you try them. I am close-minded about putting my hand in a chainsaw. It is good for me to be close-minded about this. Being close-minded is not always bad, and it is good to be intolerant of some things. You *should be* intolerant of some things.

Relativists will say you cannot impose your morality on others, that you cannot legislate your personal beliefs. But if you saw someone beating a child, wouldn't you try to stop that person? By doing so you would be imposing your morality upon him or her, but it would still be the right thing to do. Some things are right and some things are wrong, but relativists will not concede this. And doesn't all legislation impose someone's personal beliefs (or a group's personal beliefs) on the whole society? There is no moral way to sympathize with immoral actions, and it is necessary to be intolerant of some things. Besides, you don't *tolerate* things that are good, right? You don't have to. You only have to tolerate things that are unpleasant.

It is important to note that with the exception of those students fortunate enough to attend a very small group of Catholic colleges that remain faithful to Catholic intellectual life, almost every freshman college student in the country is indoctrinated in the philosophy of relativism in their first semester across almost every subject.

This subject deserves a lot more time and attention, but this is not the time or place. It was necessary for me to introduce the topic in order to make clear the importance of the next section, but I encourage you to delve more into the devastating effects of relativism and how it is reaching into every aspect of our personal and public lives.

If humanity is to make any progress in the coming century, the error of moral relativism must come to an end. And the only way to remove this insidious philosophy from our world is to root it out of our lives, one person at a time, starting with you and me. Now we come face-to-face once again with the central role that personal transformation plays in the incredible plan God has for our lives and the world. You can only rid the world of relativism by ridding individuals' lives of it one at a time. The transformation of a society and the transformation of the individuals who make up that society are inseparable. In the same way, it is impossible to transform a parish into a dynamic community without first transforming the individual members of that parish into dynamic parishioners.

The real problem with relativism is that if there is no place for truth, there is no place for wisdom. Wisdom, by definition, is the ability to discern or judge what is true, good, right, or lasting. Relativism makes wisdom irrelevant.

In the Bible we read the story of the young Solomon becoming king after his father, David, died. He was unsure of himself and concerned about his ability to lead his people. Then one night Solomon had a dream. God appeared to him and said, "Ask whatever you wish from me and I will give it to you."

If God appeared to you and said he would give you anything you asked of him, what would you request? Solomon asked for wisdom, saying to the Lord: "Give me an understanding heart to judge your people and distinguish right from wrong." (1 Kings 3:9)

Solomon asked God to give him wisdom. Wisdom is one of the goals of the Christian life. With every passing year, our ability to discern right from wrong should increase. But the world often clouds our judgment. This is another reason we need to step away from the world regularly to see how the world is affecting our judgment.

Pray for wisdom. Just as Solomon did, ask God to give you wisdom, the ability to discern what is true, good, right, and lasting.

In our own times we are woeful at distinguishing right from wrong. We have more academic degrees than ever before and plenty of knowledge, but where is the wisdom? We lust to know more and more, but we don't want to live what we already know. Wisdom is truth lived.

It takes wisdom to walk with God.

The worldview today's secular culture sets forth takes all the meaning out of life, empties life of joy, leaves us unmoored from truth and easily susceptible to manipulation, fills us with depression and despair, enslaves us, and creates an ever-present fog of confusion. On the other hand, the worldview God sets before us through the Church may bring with it great demands, but it also brings great clarity—and clarity is refreshing and liberating.

In the joy of that clarity we discover that everything in life has meaning, that every moment can be grasped for a great purpose.

Truth and deceit are all around us. Truth leads to fullness of life, and deceit seeks to rob us of that fullness of life in a thousand different ways. But we do not simply stumble into truth. Truth must be sought with humility and perseverance.

One of the most beautiful lines I have ever read is the opening of John Paul II's *The Splendor of the Truth (Veritatis Splendor)*: "The splendor of truth shines forth in all the works of the Creator and, in a special way, in man, created in the image and likeness of God. Truth enlightens man's intelligence and shapes his freedom, leading him to know and love the Lord."

If truth does shape our freedom, then without it there is only slavery. What place is there in your life for truth and wisdom? What value do you place on these things? Are you ready to begin a quest to seek truth in a new way?

The genius of Catholic teaching is that it brings clarity. We may not always appreciate the clarity that the Church delivers, but it is always better than the slavery and confusion that philosophies like relativism bring about. Seek that clarity, and when you find it, embrace it.

People Deserve Answers to Their Questions

This can all seem a little heavy, I suppose—holiness and relativism—but maybe that is just because so much in our lives has become light and superficial. It is good for us to think on serious things from time to time. It is healthy for us to ask life's big questions. Leonard Cohen observed, "Seriousness is deeply agreeable to the human spirit," and I agree with him wholeheartedly.

We live in a time of moral and ethical confusion. We live in a time that is plagued by a crisis of purposelessness. We have stopped thinking about how we should live and have given ourselves over to living however we want to live. Yet, we have failed to employ even the most basic self-observation that would have led us long ago to the conclusion that doing whatever we want does not bring us any lasting satisfaction.

The confusion of our times means that more people have more questions about Catholicism than ever before. Some of those questions get articulated, but the great majority of them remain unspoken, bouncing around in people's hearts and minds as they make their way through life. The reason so many questions remain unspoken is because most people don't know whom to ask.

Out of this situation emerges one of my firmest convictions: People deserve answers to their questions, especially questions surrounding the faith—not just generic, one-size-fits-all answers, but deeply personal answers that reach into their lives, meet them in their daily struggles and confusion, and deliver hope and clarity. They deserve answers that animate their lives in a uniquely Christian way, answers they can live.

Here we may have stumbled upon one of the most serious crises in our Church today. We live in a time when more people—Catholics and non-Catholics alike—have questions about Catholicism, but fewer people are capable of really answering those questions. Just a couple of generations ago, a child could have come home from school with a question about the Catholic faith and in the great majority of cases his or her parents would have been able to answer the question. That is no longer the case.

One thing that became abundantly clear through the research is that when you start talking to Catholics about their faith you discover an almost universal inferiority complex around how little they know about Catholicism. Most Catholics are afraid they are going to be asked a question by a colleague, a child, a relative, or even a stranger. We actually fear that wonderful grace-filled moment when someone has the courage to ask a question about our faith.

What makes Catholicism remarkably unique is that there are answers to the questions. This is part of what captured my attention when I first started to really explore Catholicism as a teenager. One of the people who challenged me to grow spiritually was a committed Catholic about fifteen years older than I, and we used to play basketball together on Thursdays. Every week he would ask me if I had any questions about the faith that I would like to talk about. I had lots of questions. One after another I would throw them at him, and he had answers to most of them. But what impressed me the most was that when he did not know the answer to a question, he would say, "I don't know. Let me look into it over the weekend and I will get you the answer next week." The first time he said this I remember thinking that it would be the last I heard of it. But the following Thursday the first thing he did was say, "So, I did some reading about that question you asked me last week, and this is what I discovered. . . ." After months of this open question forum, which was tremendously powerful in my spiritual development, one day I asked a question and he said to me, "It's time for you to go to the next level." He explained that for months he had been giving me answers to my questions, but now it was time for me to learn to find answers for myself. The following week I went to the library with the names of three books he had given me to seek out the answer to my latest question.

This back-and-forth over questions big and small had an enormous impact on my life. I learned so many lessons from the experience. Sure, I learned a lot of answers to a lot of questions I had about the Catholic faith. But that was the least of what I learned. More important, I learned how to find answers to questions that I had about the faith and developed the confidence to go looking for answers. I learned that it is not good for us to have every answer served up to us on a silver platter. It's good and healthy for us to have to go searching for the answers to some of our questions. But most of all, I learned that there are answers to our Catholic questions, and the answers are beautiful. But in order to see the beauty of the Catholic faith you have to be solely interested in seeking the truth, which means you have to set aside your own agenda and whatever prejudices life has burdened you with. The more I asked questions and the more I discovered answers, the more my confidence grew in the Catholic Church and her teachings. The questions not only led me to individual answers, but they allowed me to discover the coherent and comprehensive worldview that is Catholicism. Here I discovered that for two thousand years the best Catholic minds have been gathering wisdom on every topic that touches on the human experience, and that this gathered wisdom makes up a great treasure chest.

There are three lessons here for us: 1) Each day we need to develop our store of knowledge about the Catholic faith, so that we can live it more deeply with every passing day and so we can answer more and more questions other people have about the faith; 2) it is important that we are very clear that we don't need to have all the answers—we just need to know what resources will lead us to solid answers to Catholic questions; and 3) together as a Church, we need to get better at articulating answers to people's questions in ways that resonate with their lives.

Most Catholics have little more than an elementary knowledge of their faith. But there is something else to consider: When it comes to Catholicism there is an awful lot to know. Catholicism cannot be put on a postage stamp or broken down into a sound bite, and there is a lot more to it than just accepting Jesus as your personal Lord and Savior. It is also important to note that a seven-minute homily at Mass on Sunday is not going to make up for lost time. So how are we going to solve this problem? How are we going to help millions of Catholics of all ages learn more about the genius of Catholicism?

Learning From Highly Engaged Catholics

Dynamic Catholics can teach us an awful lot about how we can learn more about our faith. They have struggled with it in a very personal way. But the fruit of their struggle is that they have identified a path that the average Catholic can look at and say,

"I can do that!" Let's explore the traits that set highly engaged Catholics apart in this area.

It is here that we encounter Study, the second sign of a Dynamic Catholic, in a very practical way. The research revealed that highly engaged Catholics are continuous learners. On average they spend fourteen minutes each day learning more about the faith. They see themselves as students of Jesus and his Church, and they proactively make an effort to allow his teachings to guide and form them.

A number of questions emerge from these findings. Are you a continuous learner? How much time do you spend each day learning about the faith? Are you a student of Jesus? Are you a student of the Catholic Church? Do you proactively make an effort to allow the teachings of Jesus and his Church to guide and form you?

As I first reflected on these questions I realized that while the second sign is so simple, activating it in our lives requires real effort. I thought about how many days pass when I don't learn anything new about our faith. I thought about how often in my life I just make decisions without consulting God. All this led me to see that these seemingly small habits (the four signs) become incredibly powerful when applied consistently to one's life.

Paul advised the Romans, "Do not be conformed to this world, but be transformed by the renewing of your mind." (Romans 12:2) Continuous learning is the process that leads to the renewing of the mind. There is so much to discover about Catholicism. If we spent our whole lives studying it, we would still lie on our deathbeds and marvel at how little we know compared to how much there is to know. So, clearly, the meaning of life is not to learn everything there is to know about Catholicism. What we learn from Catholics with vibrant spiritual lives, who live with passion and purpose, is that learning a little bit more about our faith each day fuels our spiritual development and helps us to discover who we truly are and the plan God has for our lives.

Most of us are not called to formally study theology, but all of us are called to grow each day in our understanding of the Catholic faith. Without this, we very quickly and easily become conformed to the world.

The next thing we discover in the area of this second sign is that Dynamic Catholics have a routine for their continuous learning. Just like with prayer, they don't learn more about their faith merely when they get around to it. It has a place in their day. They have a plan. They have a routine.

Some read from a good Catholic book for a few minutes at lunchtime, or before they go to bed at night. Others listen to Catholic CDs while they are exercising. Still others listen to Catholic radio on the way to and from work each day. These are the three main forms of daily learning that the 7% identified in their lives.

Beyond their daily routine, the 7% are also significantly more likely to attend an adult education program in their parish, they are regular attendees when the parish hosts a speaker, they attend other Catholic events, and more than half of the Dynamic Catholics interviewed consider regular retreats or pilgrimages to be a powerful part of their spiritual lives.

Dynamic Catholics are hungry to grow spiritually and they thirst for the truth. The great majority of these highly engaged

Catholics have rigorously explored at least one question they've had about Catholicism. More than just asking someone about their question or searching for a quick answer on the Internet, they really threw themselves into the question or issue. This search for an answer to their most pressing question about the faith almost always brought with it two lessons. First, it is very hard to see the truth while you are in the middle of a situation, especially if the situation is highly charged emotionally. There is a certain detachment that is needed to acknowledge the truth when you do stumble upon it. We are more attached to our agendas and biases than we think. Often those agendas and biases are subconscious, so we are not even aware of how they are influencing us. Fulton Sheen wrote, "It is easy to find the truth; it is hard to face it, and harder still to follow it."

The second lesson is that disagreeing with the Church without a full examination of an issue is prideful and foolish. As I explained in introducing the second sign, even though the 7% tend to know much more about the faith than their counterparts in the 93%, they have a position of humility that is a critical element of the second sign. If they disagree with something the Church teaches, they approach the issue by exploring the question: Why does the Church teach what she teaches? They assume that it is unlikely that they know better than two thousand years of the best Catholic theologians and philosophers. They assume that they may be missing something and go searching for it. From this perspective they explore what the Church teaches to further understand God's way, eager to discover the truth. Our capacity to seek, find, and adopt truth is in direct proportion to our humility.

Engagement is one of the key concepts that impact all of the four signs. The four signs drive engagement. Not surprisingly, the more people learn about the faith the more likely they are to be highly engaged. The reverse, of course, is also true. The less you know about Catholicism the easier it is to disengage and leave. Engagement is largely influenced by a working knowledge of the faith. The exodus we have seen from the Catholic Church over the past twenty-five years is in large part an exodus of ignorance. The great majority of those who leave have no idea what they are leaving behind. It is, however, important to note that the ignorance behind this exodus is not necessarily an ignorance of doctrine, but an ignorance of application. Catholic doctrine, especially on any controversial issue, is often very well known even by non-Catholics. But most Catholics struggle to apply the Catholic perspective to the everyday moments of their lives. They lack a working knowledge of what the Church teaches.

The second sign also plays a powerful role in fueling the other three signs. Study fuels Prayer, Generosity, and Evangelization. The more we learn about our faith, the more likely we are to take the spiritual life seriously. Learning about the Catholic worldview and dignity Jesus ascribes to every human person drives Generosity. We see the Catholic vision coming together as we discover answers to questions that have been running around in our minds for some time. The natural reaction, then, is to want to share that vision and those answers with others—Evangelization, the fourth sign.

As we delve more and more into the four signs of a Dynamic Catholic, we discover that they are interconnected in powerful and practical ways, and that they really do hold the seeds for renewal in our lives and our parishes.

Now let's take a look at how we can apply the second sign to our lives. Remember, my hope is that by the time you reach the end of each chapter you will have come to understand each sign in a way that leads you to say, "I can do that!"

How Do You Eat An Elephant?

Catholicism can be intimidating. Trying to learn more about it can be overwhelming. Knowing where to start can be perplexing. To overcome the obstacles to developing a living and active knowledge of our faith, we are going to turn to one of our key concepts: continuous improvement. Continuous learning is at the heart of Study, the second sign of a Dynamic Catholic. It is a derivative of the larger concept of continuous improvement, which we discussed briefly in Chapter One. So, I thought it would be helpful to get a deeper understanding of the larger concept and how we can unleash it for powerful results in our lives and parishes.

Continuous improvement is a long-term approach that seeks to achieve small, incremental changes. Each change can be so small and simple that at the time it seems insignificant, but as you add these changes together over time they become enormous.

Consider for a moment the idea of compound interest, which is also a derivative of the overarching continuous improvement concept. Albert Einstein said, "The most powerful force in the universe is compound interest." God and love being more powerful forces, he was overstating to make his point, but he makes a good point nonetheless.

Let's look at an example to understand the power of this idea. If you set aside $100 each month for your child until she started earning a living for herself, and then she set aside $100 a month until she was sixty-five years old, there would be $78,000 saved. But if you invested that same $100 a month at a compounding interest rate of 7%, at sixty-five your child would have $1,583,822.61.

A few years ago I decided to run a marathon. The first thing I did was research how to train and prepare for the marathon. There are many different approaches, but the one I settled on was essentially based on the concept of continuous improvement. When I first started training I literally couldn't run for five minutes. But the program assured me that that was okay. The first week the program told me to run for three minutes and then walk for two minutes, alternating for forty-five minutes. As I was reading it, I thought to myself, "I can do that!" The next week I ran for five minutes and walked for two minutes. This went on, small changes each week over the course of six months, until finally I was ready to run a marathon. That's the power of continuous improvement.

Another example is writing a book. People e-mail me at least a couple of times a week asking for advice about how to write a book. The question I like to ask is, "Can you write six hundred words?"

The idea of writing a book can be daunting. My process is very simple. I decide how many chapters are going to be in the book, identify the topic for each chapter, brainstorm the key ideas for each chapter, and place them in an order that I think will flow well. Now I am ready to write. I sit down and I tell myself,

"Just write six hundred words on this idea." Anyone can write six hundred words about anything. It's nonthreatening and therefore manageable.

In the book you are reading there are six chapters. For the chapter you are reading, the structure is:

Title: The Genius of Catholicism
Section One: What's Your Worldview?
Section Two: A World Without Truth
Section Three: People Deserve Answers to Their Questions
Section Four: Learning From Highly Engaged Catholics
Section Five: How Do You Eat an Elephant?

I started off trying to write six hundred words on each of these five key ideas, and here we are six thousand words later. The idea of writing a book is overwhelming to most people. But the idea of writing six hundred words is manageable. It provides a starting point.

The hardest part of doing anything is getting started. The same is true for each of the four signs. A space shuttle uses 96 percent of its fuel during takeoff. It's getting started that is difficult. That's why we need systems. What I just described is my process for writing a book. It is a system that employs incremental improvement to help me accomplish a large task little by little. What was the first thing we identified about Dynamic Catholics? They have a daily commitment to prayer, and they have a routine of prayer. Their routine of prayer is a system that allows them to get started. What did we say about most people when they sit down to pray? They see what happens. And what happens?

Nothing, usually. They lack the routine, the system.

In any area the smallest incremental improvements can produce astounding results over a long period of time.

Several years ago I asked my team at the Dynamic Catholic Institute to ponder this question: If we had to abandon everything we are presently working on and start new projects next year, what new efforts should we turn our energy toward? The only stipulation I gave was that any idea they brought to the table had to have the potential to be a complete game changer for the Catholic Church in America. I told them we would have thirty days to think on it, and then we would meet again to discuss the ideas they had come up with. I wanted us to explore new ways of doing things that would increase our reach and the impact and sustainability of our work.

A month later we met to discuss more than sixty ideas that they had come up with. Most were dismissed quickly by the group as lacking the ability to be a complete game changer. Out of all those ideas we chose three to focus our attention on for the next decade.

The first was the research behind this book.

The second was developing the dynamic learning systems for each of the Catholic Moments: Baptism; First Reconciliation, First Communion, Confirmation, Marriage Preparation, RCIA, Advent, Lent, and Sunday Mass. We need to figure out an engaging way to teach people about the faith. What we are doing is not working. We need world-class programs in each of these areas.

The third, I must admit, I was more than a little skeptical about. The idea was to pass out free copies of the book *Rediscover*

Catholicism to everyone as they left Christmas Mass. The goal was to reinvigorate Catholics and their parishes, but particularly to make an attempt to reengage disengaged Catholics by inviting them to read a Catholic book.

"How will we pay for the books?" I asked. The team suggested we cover the cost of the pilot out of our operating budget, and if it was successful, in the future we could offer the books to parishes at a very low cost.

Have you ever noticed how full Mass is at Christmas? Thirty-two percent of the people in the pews at Christmas come to church only once or twice a year. Some come at Christmas and Easter; others for Christmas and a wedding or a baptism. The point is, at Christmas they are all there in one place, and it is the only chance we get each year to reengage them as a group. At every other time of year we have to go searching for them one at a time.

Imagine if a business knew that all their previous customers were coming together on the same day in the same place. What would they do with this information? Businesses would pull out all the stops and overcome every obstacle to find ways to reengage those customers.

If three thousand people attend Christmas Masses in your parish, that means 960 are in the once- or twice-a-year category. Do you know how difficult it is to get 960 people to come to anything? Imagine how much time, energy, and resource would be required to get 960 once-a-year Catholics to come to your church on a single day. Most parishes simply would not be able to make it happen. It would be that difficult. But once a year they show up of their own accord. Isn't it time we take full advantage of that opportunity?

Christmas is the best chance we have each year to reengage disengaged Catholics.

"How would this be a game changer?" I asked the team.

"Game changers are usually simple," a team member said. "You are always talking about how we get hypnotized by complexity when it comes to our faith because there is so much to it. But the truth is, if every Catholic in America read one great Catholic book each year, that would be a game changer. Even if the only thing Dynamic Catholics did over the next ten years was to put a copy of one great book in the hands of every Catholic in America each year, that would be an incredible contribution. But if we could establish a program that allowed parishes to distribute a different great Catholic book each Christmas, if we could make them available for, say, two dollars a copy, they could afford to give everyone a copy. Imagine what would happen if every Catholic in America read just one great Catholic book each year for the rest of their lives. It would be a game changer."

"How many Catholics read a Catholic book last year?" I asked. The answer shocked me. One percent. That's right, in 2007 only 1 percent of American Catholics read a Catholic book.

That Christmas we piloted the program with fifty thousand copies of *Rediscover Catholicism*, distributed at fifteen parishes. The response was astounding. Here are excerpts from some of the letters we received.

"I'm not sure why I came to church last Christmas. I haven't been in twenty years. But something drew me. Anyway, on the way out of church I was given a copy of your book *Rediscover*

Catholicism. For the first time in my life Catholicism makes sense to me. Thank you. I have been to church every Sunday since Christmas and all because I was handed a book."

"My son was given a copy of *Rediscover Catholicism* on the way out of church last Christmas. He stopped going to church regularly about ten years ago. We were away on vacation and I was amazed to see him reading it the next day. I was even more surprised the following week when he suggested we all go to church and then to brunch. I just want to say thank you. You don't know how happy it makes a mother to see her son return to church."

"I go to church every Sunday, but I never really got it. First I went to please my parents and then my wife, but then I received a copy of *Rediscover Catholicism* as I was walking out of Mass. Wow! I have to say, you really make it so accessible. I have given twelve people a copy of the book already, and I am not done. Thank you for the work you and your team are doing."

The Dynamic Catholic Parish Book Program has been in operation ever since. The program has been expanded to include more than a dozen books by some of the greatest Catholic authors of our time, and each year we add new titles.

This year we will distribute more than two million books and CDs for parishes to pass out at Christmas Masses. Some dioceses will distribute a book to everyone who attends Mass in their diocese this Christmas. At the request of hundreds of parishes, we also make various books available for Lent, Easter, and summer reading programs and have expanded the program to include books from many of the great Catholic voices of our time. We choose books that help people to grow in understanding and practice of the four signs and have seen incredible results in parishes, with increased engagement and enthusiasm among the early indicators.

While I agree with my teammate who said if we only distributed one book to every Catholic in America over the next ten years that would be a great contribution, we did not want to stop there. We knew we could and should do more, and the book you are holding and the research behind it is just the beginning of that bigger mission we feel called to. Much more than being just a form of learning or entertainment, books really do change our lives. We become the books we read. And the truth is, if every Catholic in America read one or two great Catholic books each year, that would be a game changer. It seems so simple, but it would change everything.

Now consider the problem at hand. Ignorance of Catholicism is massive. We are aware that the more someone knows about the faith the more likely he or she is to become highly engaged. Most people don't know where to start.

Is the solution to this problem more adult education classes or better adult education experiences? Probably not. Why? Because, even if you design the best adult education class in the world, you would still only get a fraction of the Catholic population to attend. This doesn't mean that we should not have great adult education sessions and present them in a way that is world-class. We should. They will be a game changer for some, but not for the whole Church. Is the solution to the problem better Sunday homilies? No. Why? Because you can only share so much in seven minutes on a Sunday. This doesn't mean we shouldn't work to provide world-class homilies; it just means these will not likely solve the problem of how little Catholics know about their faith. The problem with events at church is that you cannot get enough people to attend, and the problem with Sunday homilies is that they are too short and infrequent to solve the problem.

If your goal were to teach as many Catholics as much as you could about the Catholic faith over the next decade, you would need a method that was portable and practical for millions of people. The answer is good old-fashioned books.

If you read five pages of a great Catholic book every day you will be amazed how your knowledge and enthusiasm for the faith will begin to grow. Just five pages a day. I hope you're thinking, "I can do that." Five pages a day for a year is 1,825 pages in that year, 18,250 pages in a decade, and 45,625 pages over twenty-five years. That's 228 books with an average length of two hundred pages.

If you asked most people to read 45,625 pages of Catholic material, they would be completely overwhelmed. If you asked most people to commit to reading 228 Catholic books they would feel intimidated. But five pages a day, we can do that. Continuous improvement—it makes incredible things possible.

How would your life be different one year from now, five years from now, ten years from now if you read five pages of a great Catholic book each day?

How would your parish be different one year from now if every parishioner read five pages of a great Catholic book each day? How would the Catholic Church in America be different if each of us read five pages of a great Catholic book each day?

It's a game changer—simple, practical, powerful, transformative.

The world and the culture cannot answer our deepest questions or bring profound meaning to our lives. For answers to our deepest questions we must turn to God. Only then, through those answers and with an open heart, will our lives be flooded with meaning and purpose.

Five pages a day. I hope you can hear the voice of your best self within you saying, "I can do that!" If you don't know what books to start with, visit DynamicCatholic.com and request the list of ten books that changed my life. They are a great place to start. Become a continuous learner, and encourage every Catholic you know to do the same. One of the best things about Catholicism is that there are answers. Let's start to fill our hearts and minds with the truth and goodness of those answers.

How do you eat an elephant? One bite at a time.

CHAPTER SUMMARY

STUDY

- Jesus challenged the worldview of every person he encountered.
- God has an incredible dream for each and every one us. He wants you to become the-best-version-of-yourself.
- The genius of Catholicism is that everything makes sense in relation to this one idea. Whether you want to use the phrase "growing in holiness" or "becoming a-better-version-of-yourself" is entirely up to you. Life is about saying yes to the things that help you to grow in holiness (become the-best-version-of-yourself) and no to the things that don't.
- A world without truth would be a world without joy and meaning.
- Relativism is the theory that there are no absolute truths, but rather that all truth is relative. That is, something that is true for you may not necessarily be true for me. This philosophy is full of contradictions because the idea that nothing is absolute is itself an absolute statement.
- The real problem with relativism is that if there is no place for truth, there is no place for wisdom. Wisdom, by definition, is the ability to discern or judge what is true, good, right, or lasting. Relativism makes wisdom irrelevant.
- If humanity is to make any progress in the coming century, moral relativism must come to an end.
- People deserve answers to their questions, especially those surrounding the faith.
- Catholics have an almost universal inferiority complex around how little they know about their faith.
- Highly engaged Catholics are continuous learners. On average

they spend fourteen minutes each day learning more about the faith. They see themselves as students of Jesus and his Church, and they proactively make an effort to allow his teachings to guide and form them.

- Dynamic Catholics have a routine for their continuous learning. Just like with prayer, they don't learn more about their faith simply when they get around to it. It has a place in their day. They have a plan. They have a routine.

- If you read five pages of a great Catholic book every day, you will be amazed how your knowledge and enthusiasm for the faith will begin to grow. Five pages a day is 1,825 pages in a year, 18,250 pages in a decade, and 45,625 pages over twenty-five years. That's 228 books with an average length of two hundred pages.

- If you asked most people to read 45,625 pages of Catholic material, they would be completely overwhelmed. If you asked most people to commit to reading 228 Catholic books they would feel intimidated. But five pages a day, we can do that. Continuous improvement—it makes incredible things possible.

- How would your life be different one year from now, five years from now, ten years from now if you read five pages of a great Catholic book each day?

- How would your parish be different one year from now if every parishioner read five pages of a great Catholic book each day? It's a game changer—simple, practical, powerful, transformative.

- The second sign of a Dynamic Catholic is Study.

KEY CONCEPTS:

The Genius of Catholicism; the-best-version-of-yourself; Holiness; Relativism; Study; Continuous Improvement; Game Changer.

THE THIRD SIGN

GENEROSITY

Chapter Four

THE HAPPIEST PEOPLE I KNOW

THE HAPPIEST PEOPLE I know are also the most generous people I know. Is that a coincidence? I don't think so. The world proposes selfishness as the path to happiness. God proposes generosity as the path to happiness. I know many selfish people, but I don't know any who have a deep and lasting happiness. Selfish people always seem restless and discontented. The happiness we experience through selfishness is fleeting because it is dependent on external circumstances. But I also know some very generous people, and their happiness is not dependent on things going their way or on getting what they want; their happiness is rooted in the life of God. This happiness, this joy springs up from something that is taking place within them. We are all invited to that life and that happiness, and generosity is the path that leads there.

Sometimes I wonder, what is God really like? We spend a lot of time talking about God and Church, religion and spirituality, but sometimes all this talk can get in the way of us really thinking about God. Have you ever wondered what God is really like? How would you describe him? Finish this sentence: God is . . .

"God is love" is how John's Gospel finishes the sentence (John 4:8). Nietzsche made headlines with the statement "God is dead." What words would you use to describe God?

One word I would use is *generous*. In everything we attribute to God, I see immense acts of generosity. Creation is generous. Free will is generous. Life is generous. Love is generous. The generosity of God is awesome.

We find this divine generosity displayed in incredible ways by Jesus. I love to read the Gospels. I read them over and over again and always seem to catch new glimpses into the life and teachings of Jesus. The Gospels are always fresh. It's not that they change, but I change. The circumstances of my life change, the questions I am grappling with change, and so the Gospels seem new. Or perhaps it is because I wasn't open to a certain truth the last time I read a particular passage, but God has brought me to a new place, liberated me from a bias or blind spot, so now I am open to a truth that was always there. Sometimes I like to read the Gospels with one theme in mind. As I have been preparing to write this book, I have pondered the theme of generosity in the Gospels. It turns out it is a significant theme.

All the great figures that emerge in the Gospels are generous. Sure, you have the widow's mite, an obvious act of generosity. But in every great Gospel figure you find generosity. Mary's response to God when the angel appeared to her was an incredible act of faith, surrender, and generosity. The Magi, traveling from afar with gifts for the infant Jesus, were generous. The centurion begging Jesus to cure his servant was generous. The first twelve's leaving everything to follow Jesus was incredibly generous. And then there is Jesus himself. His first miracle in Cana was not a miracle of need; it was a miracle of abundance and generosity. Throughout his life he served people by teaching them, feeding them, healing them, providing spiritual leadership, and comforting them. Finally, in his suffering and death on the cross, he laid down his life for us in the ultimate act of generosity. The Gospels are a story about the triumph of generosity.

Generosity is at the heart of the Christian life, just as it is at the heart of the Gospel. For it is often through our generosity that we are able to bring the love of God to life for others in very real and tangible ways. God is by his very nature generous. God wants to convince us of his generosity, and in turn wants us to live generous lives.

But the world doesn't see it that way. Not surprisingly, again we stumble here upon the great divide between the way of life today's culture proposes and the life God invites us to live. While God is inviting us to a joyful life of selfless generosity, the world is trying to seduce us into an all-encompassing selfishness. Consider some of the differences:

God invites us to a life of gratitude while the world fosters discontent. God proposes trust; the world arouses fear. God promotes giving; the world promotes getting. God invites us to cooperate with his providence while the world rallies behind self-determinism. God appoints us in stewardship while the world touts ownership. The world encourages entitlement when in reality everything is a gift from God. God invites us to look out for our neighbor; the world tells us to look out for ourselves. God operates from abundance; the world from a place of scarcity. God created us out of generosity to live generous lives; the world encourages us to live a small, selfish life.

Generosity begins with gratitude. Are we grateful for all the blessings God has poured out upon us? In the interviews conducted with Dynamic Catholics it became obvious that highly engaged Catholics live in a state of gratitude. They have an overwhelming sense that their lives have been blessed. When I asked them to talk to me about the blessings that inspired this gratitude, they did not speak about extraordinary things. In fact, I heard nothing in those interviews that suggested that these people were any more blessed than others. But they recognized their blessings. They took time regularly to identify the people, opportunities, and possessions that brought them gratitude. It was a humbling experience for me. I realized that I have so much to be grateful for, but too often I take these blessings for granted or simply fail to reflect upon them. Am I a grateful person? There are days when I am filled with an overwhelming sense of gratitude, but on other days it is so easy to slip out of that state.

We are at our best when we are grateful. In Chapter One we spoke about spiritual health. One of the leading indicators of my own spiritual health is whether or not I am in a place of gratitude. I have observed this time and time again. When I get in a bad mood or become overwhelmed by a situation, I have usually lost the perspective of gratitude. Next time you are in a bad mood ask yourself if you are grateful. It is impossible to be grateful and be in a bad mood. It is when we step away from gratitude that we become irritable, restless, and discontented.

The world draws us into a conversation about all that we

don't have, but God invites us into a conversation about all that we do have. Which of those conversations is bouncing around your head today?

Stewardship & Providence

When we speak about generosity at church we usually do so in the context of stewardship, and we talk about three categories: time, talent, and treasure. Stewardship is the careful and responsible management of something entrusted to one's care. As Christians, we are taught that our time, talent, and treasure are all on loan to us from God—and that one day we will have to give an account for the way we managed them. The world says to do whatever you want with your time and talent, and as for your treasure—"It's your stuff!" "You earned it; it belongs to you." "What does God have to do with it?" "As for other people, let them take care of themselves." When we forget the true source of things, disorder begins to reign in our lives. God wants to lead us out of the chaos of this world and into his divine order.

Are you a good steward of what God has entrusted to you? Think about it for a moment. I know I have raised many questions in this book, but slow down, pause, and reflect upon this for a minute or two. If you consider the past twenty-four hours, were you a good steward of this time? How much time did you waste? How much time did you spend that didn't help you become a-better-version-of-yourself? Did you take time to pray? Did you give prayer your best time, when you had the energy to focus, or your worst time, when you were exhausted from another busy day?

It's humbling to think about these questions, but unless we take time to reflect on how purposefully we are approaching our role as stewards we cannot grow in this area.

Now think about your talents. Are you a good steward of the talents God has entrusted to you? Are you using them to create the most good for the most people? Are you neglecting a talent God has given you?

Are you a good steward of the treasure God has entrusted to you? Are you grateful for the money and possessions that flow through your life? Are you generous with the things you have? Do you make them available to others to enjoy, or do you guard them jealously? Are you generous with the money you have at your disposal?

In Chapter Two we spoke about the value and importance of developing a daily routine of prayer, a time each day to step away from the world and pause to spend some time reflecting on our life and commune with God. The Prayer Process set forth in that chapter allows us to pause and reflect in this way each day.

Stewardship is one of the largest responsibilities God places on our shoulders. It is impossible to live up to this responsibility unless we approach it with great intentionality. The world places many obstacles in our way as we quest to be good and faithful stewards of all God has entrusted to us.

Providence and social justice are also at the core of the stewardship discussion. As Christians we are taught that God provides for our needs. This does not mean that we can sit around, do nothing, and expect God to put dinner on the table tonight.

Providence is not an excuse for laziness. We shouldn't ask for a miracle when all that is needed is an opportunity. Providence requires our cooperation.

The central question in any discussion about divine Providence is: Do you trust that God will provide for you? Intellectually and theologically it is easy to say yes, but practically we prefer not to have to rely on God. We prefer to take things into our own hands, and that is the line that we cross to join the world's perspective of self-determinism. Part of the reason is trust, but the other part is greed. God's promise is that he will provide for our needs, not that he will provide for our greed. This is where our world collides with our neighbors'. When we place our wants before our neighbors' needs we abandon our post as stewards. There is plenty of food in the world to feed everyone, and yet more than two billion men, women, and children are hungry right now. And it is not just in foreign lands that people are hungry. More than 20 percent of children in the United States live in poverty. Mother Teresa was more in touch with human need than most. It was out of her vast experience with the suffering of so many that she counseled us, "Live simply so that others may simply live." It is sobering to think that if we were willing to go without some of the things that complicate our lives or so many of the things that we don't really need, we would be able to save lives.

My eyes always fill with tears during the scene toward the end of *Schindler's List* when the war is over and Oskar Schindler and his wife are fleeing. Having saved so many Polish Jews from certain death, he is now hunted himself. He essentially purchased his workers from a corrupt Nazi officer under the guise of needing them to work in his new factory, but in truth he was buying them in order to save their lives.

In the scene he is walking toward his car surrounded by the eleven hundred grateful Jews whose lives he saved. Now that it is over he comes to the realization that he could have done more, that he could have saved more lives. He says, "I should have sold the car, why did I keep the car? I could have got two more people." He pulls a gold pin from his jacket and says, "This is gold. I should have sold it. I could have got another person." Then Itzhak Stern, the Jew who worked with Schindler to bring all this about, grabs hold of Schindler and says, "You did so much. Look around you. Eleven hundred people are alive because of you."

Schindler was by no means a perfect man, but what he did was heroic, and still he felt he had not done enough, as if he could have and should have done more. Millions around him were doing nothing, but still he knew in his heart that he could have done more.

Today there are fewer than four thousand Jews in Poland. There are more than six thousand descendents of the Jews Schindler saved around the world.

Most of us live far from the heroic generosity of Schindler. He went to extraordinary lengths, risking his own life, to save Jewish lives during the Holocaust. But it would be a shame to come to the end of our lives and realize that we could have done so much more for others.

We cannot do everything, but that doesn't mean we should do nothing. We cannot save everyone, but that doesn't mean we shouldn't save some. Don't let what you cannot do interfere with what you can do. And what we can do, all of us, is make small sacrifices, and simplify our lives in some small ways so that others may simply live.

Once again the Gospel challenges us not theoretically, but in real and practical ways. It tries to make its way to the center of our hearts via the everyday events of our lives. I read something that caused me to pause and reevaluate my life a few weeks ago. It was something Leo XIII wrote in 1891: "Once necessity and propriety are taken care of everything else belongs to the poor." A few days later I discovered this quote from Fulton Sheen: "Never measure your generosity by what you give, but rather by what you have left." Like the rich young man, I find I have much. So each time I enter into this topic I find myself being challenged to be more generous than before.

Generosity and justice go hand in hand. If we take seriously our role as stewards of all God has entrusted to us, we will grow with every passing year to become more generous. If we are truly generous then social justice will become an integral part of who we are. When the Gospel is fully alive within us, there is no need to speak of social justice as something separate or think of it as another topic, for it is integral to the authentic Christian life. Once we immerse ourselves in the Gospel we realize that there is a level of generosity that goes beyond simply giving money and things to the poor. It is a generosity that challenges us to change the conditions that make them poor.

If we open our eyes we will discover that we are surrounded by need. The needs of others are always an invitation from God for us to live generously. Every day many prayers go unanswered, and it seems to me that this is not because God did not want those prayers answered, but because he sent us to answer those prayers and we didn't heed the call.

The Scope of Our Generosity

There are so many ways to be generous. One of my passions is reading biographies. I was reading one about Robert Redford recently, and the author had interviewed many of the actors who had worked with Redford over the course of his career as an actor and director. One of the actors described Redford as a generous director. I thought that was an interesting description. The actor went on to explain that most directors just tell you how they want a scene done and then expect you to do it that way. "But Redford would ask you to do it the way he envisioned it, and then would say, 'OK, now let's do another take and try it your own way.' It was a very generous way of directing." There is a way to be generous in everything we do.

As I examined the lives and habits of Dynamic Catholics I discovered immense generosity. In the first phase of the research, which explored volunteerism and financial contribution to their local parish, it was determined that this 7 percent of Catholics are responsible for 80 percent of the volunteer hours and 80 percent of the financial contributions in a Catholic parish. These numbers alone demonstrate that highly engaged Catholics are committed to generosity. But what really captured my attention was the variety of ways their generosity manifested itself in daily life. Generosity is a trademark of Dynamic Catholics. Their generosity in the traditional ways was to be expected. They are generous with their time and talent, with their money and possessions, but their generosity goes way beyond these commonly defined areas. It was the scope of their generosity that was particularly inspiring to me. What I discovered was not just a spirit of generosity, but a spirituality of generosity that reached deep into every corner of their lives.

Being generous is not just something that they do; it is a part of who they are. Generosity is central to their value system, and they often think in terms of how they can do the most good with what they have at their disposal.

When I spoke to their family and friends, I discovered the true depth and breadth of their generosity. Here I heard stories that nobody would ever tell about themselves.

The 7% are generous lovers, parents, and grandparents. Their neighbors and colleagues at work often acknowledge them among the most generous people they know. They are generous with their praise and their appreciation. They are especially generous in their encouragement. They are constantly encouraging people all around them. The scope of their generosity reaches into every aspect of life.

I remember one interview with a woman who had been identified by her pastor as part of the 7%. The interview was taking place in the lunchroom at her workplace, and during our time together one of her colleagues walked in. I asked the colleague a couple of questions. One thing she said provided a great insight:

"She is always looking for opportunities to be generous." Most of us are passively generous to an extent. Dynamic Catholics are proactively generous. They don't wait to be asked. They are looking for opportunities to be generous.

This all-around generosity makes them much loved by people who are close to them, as well as by people who know them just a little. It also makes them a beacon of God's love in their community.

Ask them what the source of this great generosity is and they almost always cite how blessed they consider themselves to be, and how they themselves have been the recipients of incredible generosity throughout the course of their lives. They are strikingly grateful, and it became apparent just by talking to them that their gratitude and generosity are inseparably linked.

The two forms of generosity that stood out for me, perhaps because they are so uncommon in our world today, were service and virtue. On several occasions in which the person being interviewed was in a customer service role professionally, the approach he or she described was so very countercultural.

Fabulous customer service often seems like a relic of the past, until you meet Jessica, a forty-two-year-old mother of three, working part time in a call center for a cell phone company. "People only call my department when there is a problem, so they are already frustrated. No matter how negative and angry they are, I let that just float past. I am there to help them solve their problem, and if I can do that I know I can make their day go a little smoother. It's my job and I get paid for it, but I also see it as part of my mission."

How many people who have customer service roles see it as a

part of their mission to brighten people's day by providing world-class service? Dynamic Catholics make the connection between everything they do and their faith life.

The other form of generosity that stretched me beyond how I previously thought about it was in the area of virtue. Meet Peter, a thirty-nine-year-old father of four and an executive at a Fortune 500 company. "I work hard and I work a lot. I do it because I love it and I do it to give my family a good life. But a few years ago I realized that I was losing my temper more often with my children. A few weeks later it was Christmas Eve and I had just finished building new bikes for my two eldest. I looked at all the gifts under the Christmas tree, and a hundred thoughts started racing through my mind. I never had a Christmas like my kids were about to have as a child. They don't realize how tough so many children have it. I hope we are not spoiling them. But then I started thinking about how short my fuse had been lately. I wondered, if my patience was all I could put under the tree, how would our Christmas tree look tonight? It was a defining moment in my fatherhood, and for my life. I came to the realization that it is very easy to be generous with things compared to being generous with virtue."

It is here that we stumble upon the source of our virtue: God and our relationship with him. It is said that God will never be outdone in generosity. Jesus speaks of a return of a hundredfold in this world and eternal life in the next (Mark 10:31). How generous are you with God?

I suppose it is hard to be generous with someone who has

everything and needs nothing. And yet, like any loving parent, God yearns to be with his children. God yearns to be with us. He delights in spending time with us (Proverbs 8:31). One way we can be generous with God is by spending time with him. Not just the leftovers, the scraps of our day, but dedicating a specific time each day for prayer is one way to be generous with God.

Honoring the Sabbath is another way to be generous with God. The author of Malachi poses this question: "What man would dare rob God?"(Malachi 3:8) But we do, don't we? The Sabbath belongs to the Lord, and I know from my own experience how easy it is to become preoccupied with the things of this world on Sunday. It requires a real intentionality to honor the Sabbath.

But the hardest way for us to be generous with God is by surrendering to his will for our lives. "Thy will be done, on earth." That means in our daily lives. "Thy will be done." In everything we think, do, and say. Surrendering ourselves to the will of God is the Mount Everest of spirituality and a great opportunity for each of us to be generous with God.

Every day presents an endless string of opportunities to share the love of God with other people by being generous.

How Generous Are You?

Most people think of themselves as generous, but if you get any group of people together and ask them for their time, talent, or treasure, some will be far more generous than others. The temptation is to say that those who give more money have more money, or those who volunteer more time have more time. But this is not true. Very often the busiest people are most generous with volunteering. I am often amazed at the people who volunteer to organize events in their cities for Dynamic Catholic. It takes so much time to organize a great event. So when I meet these volunteers and learn about their lives, I think to myself, "How on earth did you find time to put together such a great event?" The answer is, they didn't find time—they made time! The saying "If you want something done, ask a busy person" seems to hold true. Similarly, there are numerous studies that show that people with relatively modest incomes (and virtually no wealth) are often much more generous than those who have much more. They make giving a priority. Some people are simply more generous than others.

We are all called to live generous lives, and to grow in the area of generosity is one of the surest ways to grow spiritually. But in order to grow our generosity, we first need to get a sense of where we are today.

How generous are you? Give yourself a generosity score between one and ten, with one being the meanest, stingiest person you can imagine (think of Scrooge from Dickens's *A Christmas Carol*) and ten being the most generous person you have ever known. Circle your score on the page.

1 • 2 • 3 • 4 • 5 • 6 • 7 • 8 • 9 • 10

Now let's break it down into the three areas of stewardship that we generally talk about at church: time, talent, and treasure.

How generous are you with your time?

1 • 2 • 3 • 4 • 5 • 6 • 7 • 8 • 9 • 10

How generous are you with your talent?

1 • 2 • 3 • 4 • 5 • 6 • 7 • 8 • 9 • 10

How generous are you with your treasure?

1 • 2 • 3 • 4 • 5 • 6 • 7 • 8 • 9 • 10

Now let's consider some other areas of your life.

How generous are you in your marriage (or in your primary relationship if you are not married)?

1 • 2 • 3 • 4 • 5 • 6 • 7 • 8 • 9 • 10

How generous are you with patience?

1 • 2 • 3 • 4 • 5 • 6 • 7 • 8 • 9 • 10

How generous are you with God?

1 • 2 • 3 • 4 • 5 • 6 • 7 • 8 • 9 • 10

This simple exercise helps us to realize where we are on the spectrum of generosity. Perhaps this moment of introspection leads us to the conclusion that we are not as generous as we thought we were. On the other hand, it may bring us to the realization that even though we have been very generous in the past, we have great opportunities to be even more generous in the future. Regardless of what conclusions the exercise leads us to, one of the key lessons here is that it is important to measure things that matter.

Giving yourself a score between one and ten for your generosity is not scientific, but if you are honest with yourself and score yourself each month for a year, you will find yourself becoming more generous. Measurement creates awareness, awareness leads to intentionality, and intentionality drives behavior.

If you want to change something, start measuring it. If you want to lose weight, weigh yourself first thing every morning. Write down your weight every morning. It seems like a small thing, but what it will do is cause you to become more conscious of the foods and activities that cause you to gain or lose weight. Measurement causes us to live more intentionally.

A couple of years ago I received an e-mail from a priest. He mentioned that many of his parishioners did not make time, even a few minutes each day, to pray, and he asked if I had any suggestions. I had someone on my team design a simple card the size of a business card. On the card was listed each day of the week with a box next to it. The idea was to ask people to record exactly how many minutes they spent in prayer each day, and write it on the card. At the bottom of the card there was a box for the total number of minutes spent in prayer that week.

I encouraged the priest to pass the cards out at Mass each Sunday and ask his parishioners to record how many minutes they spent in prayer each day. They were then asked to place their cards in the collection basket with their offering the following week. After six weeks the priest e-mailed me and asked what he could do to encourage the parishioners to pray more. It was just before Lent, so I suggested he set a goal for the parish by totaling up the minutes the parish spent in prayer for the previous six weeks and coming up with a weekly average, and then setting a goal of 50 percent more.

The priest gave a homily the Sunday before Lent about how many minutes there are in a week. "There are 10,080 minutes in a week," he began, and then he went on to speak about how few of these minutes we spend in prayer before challenging the people to commit together as a parish to pray more during Lent. Finally he revealed his goal and announced that cards would be passed out at the end of Mass.

Each week during Lent he published the goal in the bulletin, and the result for the previous week. Sure enough, the number of minutes spent in prayer grew each week to meet and then far exceed the goal.

If you can't measure it, you can't change it. Measurement is key to personal growth and integral to parish growth. Certainly, there are some things that are very difficult to measure—how generous you are with your patience or forgiveness, for example. There are other things that are very easy to measure, such as how generous you are with your money. But there is something that holds all these together. It is unlikely that those who are unwilling to be generous with their patience or forgiveness will be generous with their money. Similarly, if we are not generous with our neighbor it is unlikely that we are generous with God. There may be many ways to express our generosity, but they are all interconnected and flow from one heart.

Is God calling you to live more generously? I have never asked this question and heard no as the answer. Every time I ponder this question God challenges me to a greater level of generosity—not because he wants me to give all my time, talent, and treasure away to others, but because he wants me to live a free and happy life. The happiest people I know are the most generous people I know, and they seem free from the things of this world in a way that is to be admired. Every time I think about how God is challenging me to live a more generous life, I think about the money I spend on frivolous things that I don't really need and the time I waste just being lazy. All this brings me to the realization that God is not calling me to give up something that is essential to my welfare or the welfare of my family; he is just asking me to generously dispense a portion of my excess.

But still I am resistant. Are you resistant to the generosity God is calling you to? This is one of the baffling parts of the spiritual journey. At every step God leads us into a better life than we were in before, filled with more joy, freedom, and happiness—and yet we still resist his every next step. So, what's holding you back from being more generous? Is it real or imagined?

What's holding you back from being more generous with your time? What's holding you back from being more generous with your talent? What's holding you back from being more generous with your treasure?

Pause for a moment and really ponder these three questions.

My experience has been that when we sit down and really think on these questions a little, almost everybody aspires to greater levels of generosity. The problem is life gets in the way. The demands on our time, talent, and treasure are enormous. Nurturing relationships requires endless amounts of time. Unexpected financial needs and dilemmas always seem to be popping up. It's not that people don't want to grow in their generosity; it's just that life seems to be pulling us in many directions all the time.

If we are to grow in generosity, it needs to be an intentional effort. Life is so busy and distracting. We are not going to just stumble upon greater generosity. We are pulled in so many different directions that unless we make greater generosity a priority it will not happen.

In many ways generosity is the external proof that the Gospel has taken root in our hearts. It is a lie to say that we love God if we do not love our neighbor, and generosity is at the very core of that love of neighbor. A Christian who is not generous is no Christian at all. The Gospel challenges us in ways that are difficult but profound. Time and time again we are called to give something up, but only so that we can become more perfectly who God created us to be. It is just one of the ways that Christianity invites us into a paradox. It is by giving that we receive, and even more so, it is by giving that we become.

Money – a Starting Point

How did you feel when you read the heading for this section? What was your emotional response to these four words? We tend to have strong emotional reactions to money and talk of money. So much of our hopes, fears, security, and identity can be affected by money, and so we tend to be on high alert around the subject. There is also a powerful connection between money and spirituality. When it comes to generosity, money is either a starting point or a stumbling block.

I must admit that what surprised me the most about the research surrounding the third sign was how much some of the conversations were focused on money, and not at all in the ways I had expected. But during the interviews with the 7% the reason soon became clear. I was sitting at a kitchen table in Philadelphia with one couple, Jim and Phyllis. We had been talking about generosity for some time, and then Jim said something that stopped me in my tracks: "There is a reason Jesus talked more about money than any other subject." My mind started racing, trying to verify this point. Did Jesus talk more about money than anything else? I had never really thought about it.

"Why do you think that is, Jim?" I finally managed to ask. "I cannot be certain," Jim began. "I am not a Scripture scholar, but from my own experience it seems that money has a way of getting ahold of us, and from there it can control us in ways that are so subtle that we are often not even aware of it at the time."

Phyllis added, "Money is just one of those things that can become a huge obstacle to spiritual growth."

It was one of the many powerful moments that I experienced throughout the course of the interviews. Now I decided to play the devil's advocate a bit. "But there are many ways to be generous other than with money, right?" I asked.

"Absolutely," Jim affirmed. "But if you are not generous with your money you will not be generous with your heart. In this way it is incredible how powerfully our attitude toward money can affect our relationships with our family and friends—and of course our relationship with God. Yes, there are many ways to be generous, but none of these relieve us of our need and responsibility to give financially."

One of the most common complaints about the Church is that we talk too much about money. However, I am absolutely convinced now that we don't talk enough about money. Money is so important to spiritual development that we need to talk about it much more than we do. The main issue here is that we tend only to talk about money when we are asking people to give. It is our partial treatment of the topic that rubs people the wrong way. We need to start talking about the whole money picture: giving, earning, saving, and spending. If we really want to help people grow spiritually, it is essential that we help them develop a healthy relationship with money. In fact, until we help people develop a holistic approach to money in their lives we will never really set them free to give generously the way God invites us to.

This is a perfect example of how we can meet people where they are and lead them to where God is calling them to be. Money is a part of everybody's daily life; it has a way of reaching its tentacles deep into every relationship. Fostering in people a spirituality of money is critical in today's world.

Sure, the research found that 6.8 percent of American Catholics make 80 percent of the financial contributions to parish life. But that is the effect. The cause is that highly engaged Catholics tend to have vibrant spiritual lives, deeply personal relationships with God, and a spiritual approach to money. This spirituality of money emerges from a broader philosophy of money. People who are generous with their money tend to have thought through the financial affairs of their lives. Thomas Aquinas wrote, "Grace builds on nature." In the area of money we all have a living and breathing example of this truth. The grace of giving emerges from the very practical work of formulating a budget and realizing that you earn (or have) enough to be generous with others.

Too often we talk to people about giving more money, but we don't help them develop a spirituality of money, and a day-today philosophy of money. In these circumstances, when people do give, they very often give for the wrong reasons, which is actually not very healthy for a person and can easily stunt spiritual development. When people say the Church only ever talks about money, there is often a deeper cry hidden here. Maybe this is why Jesus spoke about money so much, because he realized that in our spiritual development money is either an opportunity for growth or an obstacle to it.

Catholics will not become more generous just by being asked to give more and to give more often. They will become more generous when we help them to understand the spirituality of money and personalize it for their own lives and circumstances. If we help Catholics to develop a practical spirituality around money they will become the most generous people in the world.

The Generosity Challenge

I had my whole world rocked in this area one Sunday afternoon many years ago at a retreat. The priest leading the retreat gave a talk describing his own experience of arriving at a new parish that was in financial distress. He dreaded going to the parish from the moment he was assigned, and once he arrived became increasingly anxious about the financial situation.

One day he called another priest, who had been a longtime friend, because he just needed to talk to someone about the situation. He hoped that his friend would console and encourage him, but instead he challenged him to introduce tithing into the parish budget. "I can't pay the bills as it is, and you want me to give ten percent away?" the priest said to his friend. "You're crazy." The other priest said to him, "It seems you trust your money more than you trust God." This stung the priest right to his core, and over the next several weeks he struggled with the idea. One day he went over to the church at lunchtime and just sat in front of the tabernacle for a long time. Finally he decided that he would lead the parish to become a tithing parish.

On Monday after the Sunday collections had been counted, he went to the bank, opened a new account, and deposited 10 percent of the collections in that account. Each month for twenty years now, he has distributed 10 percent of the parish's income to various charities and ministries and to those in need. Little by little, the people of the parish were also won over to the idea of tithing. Today that parish is a vibrant spiritual community with excellent facilities and fantastic programs. It supports many ministries locally and beyond, and has a couple million dollars in the bank.

The priest finished his talk by challenging us to consider tithing in our own lives. I was thirty years old, had been a Catholic my whole life, and nobody had ever asked me to consider tithing. I was convicted as I heard his talk that day. Sure, I considered myself a generous person, but his talk challenged me to examine my financial giving, and what I discovered was that I was not particularly generous with money.

The following week I sat down and calculated what percentage of my annual income I had given to my parish and other charities over the past three years. The figure I came to was about 2 percent. Among Catholics my generosity was better than average, but nothing special. Statistically when compared with the general population I was not generous at all.

But—and we all have many buts in the area of money—the challenge to tithe seemed too much. My financial commitments at the time made it seem impossible. I read quite a bit on the subject, and many would say you had to take a leap of faith and just give the 10 percent away. Right or wrong, I was not capable of that leap of faith.

I prayed about it for a few weeks, and kept recalling the original inspiration I had found in the talk the priest had given on retreat. Finally, I came to a resolution. I would increase my giving by 1 percent of my income each year until I reached 10 percent. I laid this plan before God in prayer and I felt at peace.

Over the years, it turned out I was able to increase my giving by more than 1 percent some years. When we reached 10 percent my wife and I talked about how blessed we had been and decided that we would continue to increase our giving by 1 percent each year until it was no longer possible. This is not possible for most people. I am aware that I have been blessed more than most in the financial area. The point is each of us must prayerfully consider what God is calling us to in this area and set goals for ourselves accordingly. Recently I read about a very successful businessman who had committed to a reverse tithe—that is, each year he would live on just 10 percent of his income and give 90 percent to his church and various other charities.

The path I have taken to become more generous with money is not the only way, but it has worked for me and allowed me to grow in generosity in many different areas. By becoming more generous with money I have become more generous in my relationships and in every aspect of my life. All this is the result of one priest having the courage to challenge me to rethink financial generosity.

How much should you give? I don't know. Only you can answer that question. I know that tithing is deeply rooted in the Old Testament. The New Testament's prescription is much more difficult. Here we are encouraged to give according to what we have; the more we have, the more we should give . . . and we almost all have so much more than the people of Old Testament times.

Research conducted by the Dynamic Catholic Institute revealed that only 1.9 percent of American Catholics tithe. Research by the Barna Group shows that five percent of Americans tithe. Protestant Evangelicals are four times more likely to tithe than Catholics; 8 percent of their population tithe. In 2007, Christians in the United States gave $1,426 on average to their church and/or various other charities. When broken out as a subgroup, Catholics gave an average of $984. Non-Christians gave $905, while atheists and agnostics gave $467.

I don't know how much you should give, but here are some things to consider. How much is enough? I have never met anyone who had just enough. It doesn't seem to matter how much money we have; we always tend to think we need more. How much would you have to give away to feel it? We tend to give away a fraction of our surplus. The truth is we never really needed it to begin with. Sacrificial giving goes beyond, to a place where our giving actually requires us to go without something. How much do you have? Most of us have enough to be generous. What does God want you to do with your money? Many of us spend very little time thinking about this question, which shows that we don't take our roles as stewards seriously.

So, this is my challenge to you. I call it the Generosity Challenge. Take some time over the next week or two and calculate what you gave to your church, charities, and people in need last year as a percentage of your annual income.

Once you have that number, I challenge you to give one percent more of your income this year than you did last year. Furthermore, I challenge you to increase this giving percentage by one percent of your income each year until you reach a tithe of 10 percent (or until it simply is not possible or prudent for you to give any more). Goals bring out the best in us. We have goals for everything else; isn't it time we had some generosity goals? You will be amazed how this proactive approach to giving changes you. Now rather than waiting until you are asked to give you will be looking for opportunities to give.

As with each of the four signs, we discover that the key concept of continuous improvement can be very powerfully deployed when it comes to financial generosity.

But beyond giving, within this chapter there may be a greater call for you to have a look at the whole of your personal finances and reassess your relationship with money. Maybe it's time you had a budget! Perhaps there are some other practical money matters that need your attention in order for you to be a good steward. We don't just stumble into a life of financial generosity. It requires intentionality. Without an intentional plan around money and giving, it is too easy for money to get a grip on us.

We have covered a lot in this section and in this chapter. What is critical is that you don't get overwhelmed. Break it down into manageable pieces, so that you can say, "I can do that!"

The Most Generous People You Know

Who are the most generous people you know? Ask someone this question and you will more than likely hear an inspiring story. When I reflect on this question there are two groups of people that immediately come to mind, who have had an enormous impact on my work over the past twenty years. Every year I am more grateful for these people, without whose generosity I would never have been able to reach as many people as I have.

The first are event organizers. When I arrive at an event I am intensely aware that the planning for that event began about twelve months earlier. For almost a year this group of dedicated volunteers has been working tirelessly to make this event a success. When I meet people on the organizing committee I often wonder to myself, "How did you have time to organize this event?" Like most people today, they have very busy lives filled with lots of commitments and responsibilities. Their generosity is inspiring.

The other group that immediately comes to mind when I think about the most generous people I know is the Ambassadors' Club. This is the most inspiring group of people I know.

These are the faithful members who drive almost everything we do at the Dynamic Catholic Institute. Each ambassador commits to giving a monthly donation to support our work. Last week at an event a man told me that he had decided to give up cable television and give the money to us instead. He explained that at first it was the hardest thing he had ever done, but now, a year later, it is the best thing he has ever done. He went on to explain how it had changed his life: "My marriage is better than it has ever been. I'm a much better father. I am really growing spiritually for the first time in my life. It's amazing—just because I am watching less television."

Everywhere we turn there is generosity. The daily generosity of parents and the sacrifices they make for their children; the incredible generosity of our priests, men who give their lives to serve God's people and lead them spiritually; the courageous generosity of all those who serve in the military; and humanity's constant efforts to relieve the suffering of the poor and the marginalized. And still, it is so easy for us to selfishly focus on ourselves. But with every passing day, God is gently inviting us to live more generously, calling us to switch the focus off ourselves and onto others.

"It is better to give than to receive." (Acts 20:35) The more we are mindful of how much we have received, the more we are inclined to look for opportunities to give. God is the supreme giver, and whenever we give we grow in the image of God, become a-better-version-of-ourselves, and live holy lives.

"May our love for you express itself in our eagerness to do good for others." This is the opening prayer for Mass from the twenty-eighth week of Ordinary Time. Notice the wording. We are not called to give begrudgingly. It is not even a willingness to do good that God calls us to. Far above these, when we are at our best as human beings, we are filled with an eagerness to do good, an eagerness to give generously, and an eagerness to help our brothers and sisters regardless of what ocean or idea separates us.

May God bless us all with an eagerness to live generously.

CHAPTER SUMMARY

GENEROSITY

- The happiest people I know are also the most generous people I know.
- God is generous, and generosity is at the heart of the Christian life.
- Generosity begins with gratitude.
- Dynamic Catholics live in a state of gratitude. They have an overwhelming sense that their lives have been blessed.
- The world draws us into a conversation about all that we don't have, but God invites us into a conversation about all that we do have. We are at our best when we are grateful.
- When we speak about generosity at church we usually do so in the context of stewardship, and we talk about three categories: time, talent, and treasure. Stewardship is the careful and responsible management of something entrusted to one's care. As Christians, we are taught that our time, talent, and treasure are all on loan to us—and that one day we will have to account for the way we managed them.
- Don't let what you can't do interfere with what you can do.
- Generosity is a trademark of Dynamic Catholics. They are generous with their time and talent and with their money and possessions, but their generosity goes way beyond these commonly defined areas. They have not just a spirit of generosity, but a spirituality of generosity that reaches deep into every corner of their lives. Generosity is central to their value system, and they often think in terms of how they can do the most good with what they have at their disposal.
- The 7% are generous lovers, parents, and grandparents. Their

neighbors and colleagues at work often acknowledge them among the most generous people they know. They are generous with their praise and their appreciation. They are especially generous with their encouragement. They are constantly encouraging people all around them. The scope of their generosity reaches into every aspect of life.

- Establish giving goals. Give one percent more of your income this year than you did last year to your church and favorite charities. Increase this giving percentage by one percent of your income each year until you reach a tithe of 10 percent (or until it simply is not possible or prudent for you to give any more). Goals bring out the best in us. We have goals for everything else; isn't it time we had some generosity goals?

- The third sign of a Dynamic Catholic is Generosity.

KEY CONCEPTS:

Generosity; Stewardship; Divine Providence; Tithing; Money; The Generosity Challenge; Giving Goals.

THE FOURTH SIGN

EVANGELIZATION

Chapter Five

CHANGING THE WORLD

IMAGINE FOR A MOMENT that by some mysterious power you were able to change the world. What would you change? How would you change it? Superheroes use their power to outwit the bad guys. When songwriters assign themselves the power to change the world they often use it to win the love of the one they desire. Getting rid of the bad guys is certainly fine and noble, as is love, but surely if we could change the world we should use that power for the greatest impact.

How would you change the world? Perhaps you would eradicate poverty, disease, and ignorance, or put an end to war, famine, and all the useless violence and destruction that we inflict upon each other.

But changing the world is an inside-out job. When we look to change the world, too often we look outside ourselves. When God looks to change the world, he looks deep within us, driving straight to the heart of the matter: human behavior. The world is the way it is today because of human behavior. The world is changing, constantly, for better or for worse. The way we live our lives today makes it better or worse tomorrow. There are seven billion people on the planet. If your life were multiplied by seven billion, what would the world be like?

For the Prologue I used a story that I have been telling since I first began speaking: If you get the man right (and the woman, of course) you get the world right. The world only changes for the better when men and women grow in virtue and character. Less virtue can never lead to a better world. Less character will never lead to a better world. Our lives genuinely improve only when we become better people today than we were yesterday; the destiny of the world is wrapped up in this deeply personal quest.

In the book of Exodus we read the story of Moses leading the people out of slavery and into the promised land. God wants to do the same for each and every one of us. He wants to lead us out of our slavery, whatever that is for you and me, and lead us to the promised land of a life filled with passion and purpose. But along the way, despite the incredible things the Lord had done for the Israelites, they turned away from God, became discontented and filled with entitlement, and began to argue among themselves and divide as a community.

What did God do? He offered them a fresh start, just as he offers each of us a fresh start today. But that fresh start was not based on ideas or philosophies. It was based on a new way of living. God invited them to change the way they behaved. He essentially said, Live by these Ten Commandments I place before you today and you will live rich, full lives in friendship with me . . . and the world will be a better place for everyone. It is amazing how timeless those commandments are.

1. You shall love the Lord your God and serve him only.
2. You shall not take the name of the Lord your God in vain.
3. Keep holy the Sabbath.
4. Honor your father and your mother.
5. You shall not kill.
6. You shall not commit adultery.
7. You shall not steal.
8. You shall not bear false witness.
9. You shall not covet your neighbor's wife.
10. You shall not covet your neighbor's goods.

I know it may seem a little old-fashioned, but wisdom is always old-fashioned. Let me suggest a small exercise. Watch the news tomorrow night with this list in front of you. As each story is presented, usually misery after misery, consider which of these ten have been broken. In the great majority of cases, wherever you find injustice and misery in this world you find that at least one of the Ten Commandments has been broken.

Imagine all of the misery that could be avoided if we all just lived by these ten nuggets of life-giving wisdom. Think for a moment on all the suffering that is caused because humanity has been unwilling to adopt a pattern of behavior and a social structure that celebrates the wisdom of the Ten.

The world needs changing, today as much as ever before. Most people agree the world is a bit of a mess. I don't know anyone who would say it is in great shape, on the right track, changing unequivocally for the better. Parents seem universally concerned about the world their children will grow up in. When I speak with grandparents, they often tell me that they don't like to think about the world their grandchildren will inherit because it makes them too anxious.

Sure, we have explored space and invented the Internet, but one-third of the world's population is starving and the moral-ethical foundation of our society is being demolished before our very eyes. We have more and more of what we want, but less and less of what we need.

The world is a bit of a mess, but we abdicate the responsibility for this in two ways: We convince ourselves that the state of the world is someone else's fault, and we convince ourselves that it's someone else's responsibility to fix. We are wrong on both counts. Even sadder is the fact that more and more people believe that the world cannot get better. The truth is we are all changing the world. Every word, thought—yes, even your thoughts—and action changes the world in ways that echo throughout the world, touching people and places you will never meet, for ages to come.

Most people agree the world is a bit of a mess, but as Christians we refuse to believe that it must be so. We believe something can and should be done about it, and that we are called to play an active role in the transformation that is so obviously needed. We are called to be especially mindful of the role we play in changing the world.

This is particularly true for Catholics. Our mission as Catholics is not merely to move through the world, leaving it unchanged. Changing the world is part of our mission, and throughout history we have done that in many ways. The Catholic Church broke the class barrier for education. We invented the scientific method to transform the sciences. We have always been a leader in caring for the sick and the poor. In almost every place and time for the past two thousand years, the Catholic Church has played a powerful role in making the world a better place. Catholics change the world.

It is, however, important to remember with heavy hearts that our influence has not always been positive. Catholics have affected the world in horrible ways also: the persecution of Galileo, the burning at the stake of Joan of Arc and others, the atrocities of the Inquisition, the persecution of so many saints, and the sexual abuse scandal within the priesthood. But even in the face of these horrific contributions to history, it is impossible to argue that the Catholic Church has not been a force for good around the world for two thousand years. It is also important to note that when we have failed it has always been because we did not live our Catholic faith authentically.

Imagine for a moment if the Catholic Church had never existed. Could you even count the number of people throughout history who would have starved to death, the number of people who would never have been educated? How could you measure the influence of all those the Church has raised up? How do you measure every kind word of encouragement and good deed that has been inspired by the Catholic faith? Can you even imagine removing all these from human history? And if we could, what kind of a world would we find ourselves in today?

There are a growing number of people who think the world would be a better place if the Catholic Church had never existed. I pray you and I can live lives that discredit this argument more and more with every passing day.

Changing the world, now that is something worth getting excited about. But how often do you walk into church and think to yourself, "This is a group of people focused on changing the world"? I have been around groups of people who were trying to change the world in small ways and I have been around those who were simply trying to change their business or industry, and I can tell you that the energy that those groups of people exert is very different from the energy we exude as Catholics at the moment. It may be an oversimplification, but the reason for so many of our problems and inefficiencies at this moment may be that we have forgotten that we have been commissioned to change the world.

This is part of our great mission. But we seem to have lost sight of it in so many ways, and we seem obsessed with maintenance and survival. Mission or maintenance? This is the question that our times are laying at the feet of the Catholic Church. I hope with all my heart that we choose to mobilize around our great mission once again.

Nothing drives engagement like a worthy mission, and we certainly have that.

Imagine what we could achieve if we mobilized. There are seventy-seven million Catholics in the United States today. Catholics could determine every presidential election in this country. We could direct the outcome of almost every election at any level in this country. Catholics could determine the success or failure of almost any product or company. We could direct legislation, influence the types of movies that are made, control the nature of television programming that is produced, and put an end to poverty in America. If we could get our act together . . .

But instead, the last remaining socially acceptable prejudice in America is to be anti-Catholic. In our hypersensitive, politically correct culture, which preaches tolerance as the ultimate twenty-first-century virtue, everything is tolerated from the perverse to the insane, but not Catholicism. Tolerance is extended to all except Christians and their beliefs. These are seemingly intolerable.

We need to wake up. We have been fooled into believing that we are some quirky little fringe group. We can and should be a force to be reckoned with. Why do you think we are attacked so much? Those who oppose the Catholic worldview are afraid of how much influence we would have if we did ever actually get our act together.

And while it is important that we consider our worldly influence, and it is critical that we do get our act together in this respect, it is also crucial that we don't make these things an end in and of themselves. The worldly influence we are called to exert can so easily distract us from our primary mission of helping people discover God and walk with him.

So changing the world temporally is not the primary way we are called to exert our influence. I use worldly examples to demonstrate what is possible. But we need to focus first and foremost on becoming men and women of virtue and character, and leading others to do the same. Every good thing we hope for the world will flow from the reemergence of character and virtue in our lives and in society.

The Best Way to Live

How is the best way to live? Every great civilization has concerned itself with this question. It is the primary question that the great philosophers of every age have grappled with. It is the question every culture, country, generation, and individual (consciously or unconsciously) wrestles with. It is one of the questions that are at the core of any spiritual quest. But perhaps most important, it is a question you and I grapple with in a deeply personal way at every juncture of our lives.

The rigor with which a person or culture approaches this question is very telling. It is of disturbing importance to note that the present culture has virtually no interest in pursuing it. Today we are more interested in how we want to live than we are in discovering the best way to live, just as we are much more interested in defending self-expression than we are in developing selves that are worth expressing. Personal preference has triumphed over the pursuit of excellence. We want what we want, and we feel entitled to it.

But the question remains: How is the best way to live? Though perhaps we need to consider another question in order to come to fully answer this one: Are some ways of living better than others? Our hyper-relativistic culture says no. We are told that the best way to live is different for every person, but that is only partially true.

Certainly we cannot consider this question in a vacuum. It must be pondered in a real place and time, for a specific person, with roles and responsibilities, needs, hopes, and desires. With this in mind we tend to leap straight to the conclusion that the best way to live is different for everyone. But is it? The answer, I think, is yes and no. A more strategic approach to this ageless question should consider what is common to everyone before we leap to what is unique to each individual.

On some level the best way to live is the same for all of us. Let us consider these three principles that are common to all men and women of goodwill.

THE FIRST PRINCIPLE. The First Principle is simply this: You are here to become the-best-version-of-yourself. Surely we can all agree that you are not here to become a-second-rate-version-of-yourself, that it is better to explore your potential than to squander it. Nor are you here to be another version of your parents, teachers, friends, or siblings. At some very basic foundational level God has created you and put you here on earth to be yourself. But being yourself is much more difficult than most would suppose, because it requires the real work of self-discovery. It also requires that you die unto your lesser self, so that in Christ your better self can emerge. Nonetheless, in this you share a common bond with all men, women, and children, for we are all here to become the-best-version-of-ourselves. The best way to live, therefore, is in ways that help you become the-best-version-of-yourself.

This first principle serves not only as a basis upon which to begin to answer the question about the best way to live but also as a very practical guide to the choices that make up everyday life. In fact, I would go so far as to say that everything in life makes sense in relation to this single principle. Embrace everyone and everything that helps you become a-better-version-of-yourself and you will live a life uncommon.

Everything makes sense in relation to the first principle. Life is about saying yes to the things that help you become the-best-version-of-yourself and no to the things that don't. It is not more complicated than that. Of course, we manage to complicate life substantially more. On a different plane of thinking the concept becomes a thing of beauty, for we finally realize that anyone or anything that does not help us to become a-better-version-of-ourselves is just too small for us. What liberation and joy we experience when we make this truth our own for the very first time.

This concept of celebrating the-best-version-of-ourselves at each moment and in each situation throughout the day brings the philosophical question "How is the best way to live?" to a very real and practical level. As our awareness grows we become mindful that we are constantly making choices and that every choice causes us to become a-better-version-of-ourselves or a-lesser-version-of-ourselves.

It is a natural extension that the best way to live also includes living your life in ways that help others to become the-best-version-of-themselves. Whenever we cause others to become a-lesser-version-of-themselves we are not at our best, and we are not living our best possible life. To prevent someone else from becoming the-best-version-of-themselves—now, that is a sin.

If we accept the first principle then the meaning-of-life conversation becomes a fairly short one. You are here to become the-best-version-of-yourself. It is by knowing, loving, and serving

God and neighbor that we become all he created us to be. We all have this in common, and so the best way to live on a macro level is the same for everyone. We are here to become the-best-version-of-ourselves. And so on one level the answer to the question "How is the best way to live?" is the same for us all.

THE SECOND PRINCIPLE. As we continue to explore the best way to live, we will discover that it is not as different from person to person as one might first think. For thousands of years great minds including Plato, Aristotle, Augustine, Aquinas, Duns Scotus, Descartes, Immanuel Kant, Marcus Aurelius, Epictetus, and others have each in their own way held that "virtue" is the best way to live.

Every culture, country, and organization has an organizing principle. For Hitler's Germany it was tyranny. For China it is Communism. For Castro's Cuba it is dictatorship. For the United States it is law, which supports democracy and capitalism. For many companies it is reward. For some organizations it is excellence or contribution. For others it is fear.

But what is the ultimate organizing principle—for your life, your family, an organization, a country, or indeed, the whole world? Virtue. Not necessarily in a religious sense, but simply in the classical Greek sense of the word.

Consider this. Two patient people will always have a better relationship than two impatient people. Two generous people will always have a better relationship than two selfish people. Two courageous people will always have a better relationship than two cowardly people. Two humble people will always have a better relationship than two prideful people. And every aspect of society—a family, a community, an organization, or even foreign relations between two nations—is an extension and multiplication of this single relationship.

Think of it this way. Who would you prefer as your employees or colleagues—men and women of virtue or those riddled with vice and selfishness? Would you prefer your neighbors be patient or impatient? Would you rather your extended family were generous or self-serving? Would you prefer honest or dishonest customers? Would you rather have a courageous or a cowardly manager?

The whole world prefers virtue.

Our present culture likes to say that virtue is a personal matter. Indeed, in some ways it is, but the impact of the virtue (or lack of virtue) of any one person cannot be confined to that person. Our words and actions, though personal, have real consequences on the lives of other people. These consequences are never confined to the individual. If one man shoots another man, the shooter's actions impact not only the man who is shot but also that man's wife and children, his mother and father, brothers and sisters, friends and neighbors. Every good thing he may have done for the rest of his life will go undone. He may have been the person who was going to cure cancer. In the same way, if you help someone to find a job, your loving actions help that person, but also his (or her) family and the local community in so many ways it is impossible to measure. There are no purely personal acts. Everything we say, do, and think affects other people.

Virtue is the ultimate organizing principle, whether it is in a person's life, a marriage, or the life of a nation. And so, in virtue, we have another example of how the best way to live is the same for us all.

THE THIRD PRINCIPLE. The third principle is simply self-control. The best way to live is with self-control, which may very well be man's highest need. Without it we are rendered incapable of any sustainable success in life, business, relationships, or spirituality. For without self-control we are incapable of delaying gratification. Individualism, hedonism, relativism, and minimalism, the dominant practical philosophies of our age, all lead to the decay of humanity's self-control and the demise of our ability to delay gratification.

There is no success without the ability to delay gratification. What happens to someone's personal finances if they cannot delay gratification? What type of relationships is a person likely to have if he or she is unwilling to delay gratification? What quality of work can you expect from a person who is unable to delay gratification? What will happen to the health and well-being of a person who refuses in every instance to delay gratification? And you simply cannot grow spiritually if you refuse to delay gratification.

To be clear, I am not saying that we should always delay gratification. God wants us to experience intense pleasure. I am simply saying that in order to live your best life the ability to delay gratification is a required skill. And although there is more to self-control than delayed gratification, the two are inseparably linked. A person who is unable to delay gratification is incapable of self-control. If you wish to increase your self-control and create a stronger mind and more resolute will, practice delaying gratification many times a day.

It is better to live with self-control than it is to live without it. Here we have another example of how the best way to live is the same for us all.

So to recap: 1) You are here to become the-best-version-of-yourself; 2) virtue is the ultimate organizing principle; and 3) self-control is central to the best way to live. In these three principles we find the common elements that bind us all together in our quest to answer the question "How is the best way to live?" It is better to live in a way that helps you become the-best-version-of-yourself than to live in a way that diminishes you and makes you less than who you are. It is better to live a life of virtue than a life of vice. And it is better to live with self-control than without it.

It is also important to note that most people's knowledge of and dedication to these three principles is minimal. At the same time most people's dedication to the philosophies of individualism, hedonism, relativism, and minimalism dwarfs their commitment to these three principles. Therein lies the challenge for anyone who wants to change the world.

It is true, however, that the answer to the question is in some ways different from person to person, and it changes for an individual at different times of his or her life.

The best way for a single person to live may legitimately be very different from the best way for a married person to live. One of my passions is helping young people discover their mission in life. When I have the chance to speak to high school and college students, one of my regular themes surrounds embracing "singleness."

We never have a better opportunity to serve than when we are single. Most people go on to marry, and marriage brings with it a series of commitments and responsibilities that limit our ability to serve people, causes, and organizations beyond our immediate duties. But in our singleness we can serve generously almost without reserve and in ways that would not be possible for a married person.

On a personal level, when I was single the best way for me to live was to be actively involved in a variety of community and charitable organizations. Now that I am married and raising my family, I would be irresponsible as a husband and father to be involved in all these volunteer activities to the same extent. It would not be the best way to live, because it would be giving priority to something that is secondary. My primary responsibilities now are as a husband and a father.

In the same way, the best way to live can change as we move through the various seasons of life. What is the best way to live at twenty years old may differ at forty, fifty, or sixty. This is true even though our primary roles and responsibilities may not change in these different stages of life.

And so by delving into the question of the best way to live, we quickly discover that it is not a question that we ask once, answer once, and are finished with. It is a dynamic question that requires a little bit of our attention every day for the rest of our lives.

Jesus was essentially asked this question once. One day while he was teaching in the temple he was approached by some of the religious leaders of his time. In an attempt to trick him, they asked him which was the greatest of the commandments. Jesus replied, "Love the Lord your God with all your heart, with all your soul, and with all your mind . . . and love your neighbor as yourself." (Matthew 22:37–39) And in doing so he also answered the question "How is the best way to live?"

The entire Gospels are an expanded answer to this question. In a sense every person who approaches Jesus is looking for the best way to live, just as you and I are constantly seeking the best way to live whether we are conscious of it or not.

The life of the Church and her teachings are an extension of the Gospel in that they too try to lead us toward the best way to live. As the ages have unfolded, new situations and questions have arisen, and men and women of goodwill have come to the Church and asked, "How is the best way to live in respect to this particular circumstance?" These answers all come together into an incredible body of knowledge and wisdom and are available to all people of all times.

Often people think that the Church says you have to do this or you cannot do that. In fact, the Church does no such thing. The Church simply stands in every place and time pointing out the path toward the best way to live. Each of us gets to decide if we are going to walk that path or not.

And this is where we get to the heart of the matter. It is here that a new question arises: Do you believe that Jesus offers us the best way to live? If you don't believe that the life, teachings, and person of Jesus lead to the best way to live, who or what does? If you do believe that Jesus leads us in the best way to live, then isn't it a natural consequence that you want to share that best way with others? And that is Evangelization—helping them to discover the love of God and the wisdom of his ways; helping people to live their best possible life and become the-best-version-of-themselves, helping people to discover the best way to live.

We want these things for anyone we love.

Jesus invites us to a life of love. How much do we really love? Sure, we love the people close to us. But most of the time, the giving and receiving go on in equal measure in these relationships. How often do we love and expect nothing in return? How often do we do something out of love that requires us to make sacrifices?

Evangelization is the ultimate form of love of neighbor. Is there any greater way to love your neighbor than by helping him or her discover the best way to live?

Are some ways of living better than others? Our relativistic culture says all ways of living are equal, but this is nonsense. We are told in this age of secularism that we should respect everybody's right to live however they wish, but how is that working out for us? Isn't this already a failed experiment? Relativism leads to a world where nobody is the-best-version-of-themselves. Were Mother Teresa's approach to life and Hitler's approach to life equal? I think not. One was better than the other. Relativism is the enemy of Evangelization, because if all ways of living are equal then there is no need to lead others to a better life. Even the most casual observer comes to the conclusion upon reflection that some ways of living are better than others, and if that is the case, then there must be a best way of living. And if some ways of living are better than others, shouldn't we do what we can to help as many people as possible discover the best way to live?

I find it fascinating that we almost never talk about Heaven and hell anymore. What do you think happens when we die? Do you believe in Heaven? I do. My reasons are not as theological as some might expect. You see, I believe that this life is just a dim reflection of some infinitely greater reality. In my life I have experienced moments of incredible ecstasy—finding the person to spend my life with, the birth of my children, and to a lesser extent moments in travel, standing before truly beautiful art, a perfect golf shot—but these moments are fleeting and impossible to hold on to. Nonetheless, I believe they provide a glimpse into what God has in store for us, a preview of sorts. I have also experienced the love of God and the love of others, and if I reflect on what it would be like to be constantly in those moments of incredible love it is not difficult for me to imagine what Heaven might be like. And yet, I know that whatever I can imagine is only a dim reflection of what actually is. My faith counsels me that no one is disappointed when they experience Heaven.

For the same reasons, I believe in hell. I have tasted this experience too. There have been moments of great darkness in my life, when evil felt all too close. More to the point, I have felt far from God at times. I have also witnessed other people who were possessed by a living hell on earth. And as horrific as these dark moments can be—in our own lives or as we witness them in the lives of others—I also believe that these are just a dim reflection of an infinitely darker reality.

And while we are at it, we might as well take a moment to discuss the concept of purgatory. I am a practical man. If I eat too many doughnuts or french fries, I gain weight. In order to return to optimal health, I then have to exercise vigorously and abide by a rather strict diet. It would seem to me that the same is true spiritually. If I indulge in a vice on a regular basis my spiritual health is diminished. This vice affects my spiritual and physical health, my relationships, my intellectual clarity, and many other aspects of life, most of which I am probably not even aware of. Perhaps one day I decide to stop partaking in that vice. I may stop today, but the effects of my previous bad behavior will live in me for some time to come. It is only by the consistent and persistent practice of virtue that I may over time do away with the residual bad effects of my previous life of vice.

Now consider, what is Heaven? We may all have different ideas, but most can agree that it is a perfect state or experience. If you place something that is imperfect in something that is perfect, the whole becomes imperfect. For example, if you have a glass of pure olive oil and you add a drop of motor oil, you no longer have a glass of olive oil. I'm not sure what you have, but it is not olive oil. The glass of pure olive oil is Heaven; the drop of motor oil is something less than perfect—you and I. We can probably agree that most people are not the-best-version-of-themselves when they die, and so purgatory (an experience of purification) is just a natural and necessary consequence. Otherwise, adding something imperfect to something that is perfect would diminish it all.

When we do get to Heaven I suspect there will be many surprises. Among these surprises, I think most people will be astounded to learn how much they are loved and how lovable they are. But we digress. If Heaven does exist, don't you want as many people as possible to experience it?

Win, Build, Send

Imagine you discovered the best way to live and you wanted to change the world by helping as many people as possible to discover and live that best way. How would you go about it? Anyone who has any experience in marketing products or ideas will tell you that you need a system, and the best systems are simple. As it turns out, God has had a system in place from the very beginning. God wants to *win* you with his love and wisdom; God wants to *build* you up spiritually so that you have the knowledge and habits to live in his love and walk in his ways; and God wants to *send* you out into the world to share his love with others. *Win. Build. Send.*

God's plan for changing the world is to get as many people as possible to live the Gospel, which as we have just discovered turns out to be the best way to live. But first and foremost he desires a dynamic and intimate friendship with us. Think about that. We are talking about the Creator of the universe here. If the President of the United States, the future King of England, or your favorite celebrity wanted to have a dynamic friendship with you, you would be flattered and enthusiastic. God wants to have an intimate friendship with you.

WIN

As I began to explain in the previous chapter, when I was about fifteen years old I was tremendously fortunate that a handful of people helped me discover the genius of Catholicism. I really don't know where I would be today, or what I would be doing, if they had not taken the time to help me develop spiritually. My story is not as dramatic as others'; it is simply a story of dissatisfaction with the life and ideas that the culture was serving up. It was a classic case of "there must be more to life."

One of the most intriguing things about Catholicism is that once you get a taste of the real thing it is absolutely fascinating and incredibly beautiful. Looking back I think I was won for Christ and his Church by a single idea: We are all called to live holy lives. Of course, I was not won the first time I heard the idea. On paper it seems like an intimidating concept, but this became an organizing thought. Everything seemed to fall into place around this idea. There were certain ways to think, speak, and behave that caused me to grow in goodness, virtue, and holiness. There were other ways to think, speak, and behave that did not. This just seemed like common sense to me when I was encouraged to think about it. I had simply never been encouraged to think about it in such a compelling way. No great leap of faith was required. On a very natural level it seemed logical and practical.

From a purely selfish point of view I noticed that when I was walking with God and living the life he invites us all to live through the Gospels, I was happier. Happiness and holiness are intimately connected. In fact, I would go so far as to say that you cannot have one without the other. The connection between right action and human happiness was unmistakable to me even as a teenager. I also noticed that the more I tried to live the life God was inviting me to, the more I became genuinely myself. And so you can see where the phrase "the-best-version-of-yourself" came from. It is simply an attempt to put into the language of our age the dream that God has for all his children: that we grow to become all he created us to be.

It is also important to point out that I was not won once and for all. None of us are. We are human beings and as such we tend to vacillate, sometimes even in our most noble convictions. We are constantly engaging and disengaging. We go to and fro, even in important matters. Our love and allegiance, unlike God's, are not constant. At times I am filled with great doubts about aspects of our faith, while at other times I am filled with an almost absolute faith. There are times when I am on the verge of depression thinking about how human weakness in the Church has devastated the faith of so many people. At other times I am supremely confident that God is guiding all things in the life of the Church.

Just when I think I cannot love my wife any more than I already do, she will win me in new and unexpected ways, and it can be the simplest things that raise my love to a new level. I saw her reading to our daughter the other day. Isabel is just nine months old, but she loves having books read to her. She was so animated as Meggie read to her, and I thought to myself, what an incredible mother she is. In the same way, God wins me anew time and time again. There are things that happen every year that cause me to fall in love with his way more than ever before. What I am trying to say is that God does not win us just once. He wins us over and over again, in new and deeper ways. It is important that we understand this; otherwise we can fall into the trap of thinking that the Win, Build, Send model is a one-time progression. This would leave us susceptible to saying that because we have not yet been won or built completely we are not ready to be sent. Some of the smartest people I know get completely trapped in the win stage, and go around and around in circles for years. Others resist the send stage, saying that they have not been built sufficiently yet. The build and send stages will win you in new ways.

The biggest challenge I have faced in writing this book has been in trying to work out who the reader would be. Who are you? Man? Woman? Young? Old? Single? Married? Priest? Are you at the all-important moment in your life when you are searching for some clarity in the area of your faith? Are you hungry to grow spiritually? Are you already a highly engaged Catholic? Or perhaps you are a priest looking for solutions to the many complex challenges you face every day in the life of your parish. I don't know who you are, but I am not sure that matters. As long as you are willing to explore this question: Has Christ won you?

For most people the answer is in degrees. Most of us have been won to some extent. The question then becomes whether we are willing to let Jesus win us in new ways. I won't say I am completely won, although I hope eventually he wins me completely. If we allow him to win us over to his life and love a little more this year than last year, that is progress, spiritual progress—and that is a beautiful thing. Progress is never to be scoffed at, however slight it might be.

There are three ways people are won: through truth, beauty, and goodness. For some people it is the truth that shines forth from an intellectual search that wins their hearts for God. They read Thomas Aquinas and the beauty of truth and logic wins them over. For others it is the beauty of the Sistine Chapel or Chartres cathedral that wins their hearts for God. And for others still, it is the goodness of Christian service that wins them, when they witness Mother Teresa caring for an AIDS patient or they experience the goodness of Christian friendship, a friendship that has the other person's best interest at its core. Most of us are won by a combination of all three.

What's important to note is that if you examine the history of our faith and study the stories of millions of people who have come to a greater appreciation of Catholicism, while every person's story is unique, they have all come to Jesus through one of these three paths—truth, beauty, and goodness.

Among the highly engaged Catholics who were interviewed as part of this research, 89 percent described a conversion experience—an event in their life that won them to a more engaged relationship with God. Some of them used this language and described it as a conversion, but many of them described it with other language. Some simply said things such as, "That was when I really got it for the first time!" Some "got it" by going on a retreat, on a pilgrimage, or to a conference, others got it by reading a book or listening to a CD, and still others got it when they experienced a life-altering event or the death of a loved one.

We all need at least one really good conversion in our lives. But conversion is an ongoing process in the life of a Christian.

This I know for sure: We need to work out what exactly is the best way (or ways) to win modern Catholics for Jesus and his Church. It is clear when you talk to highly engaged Catholics that they get it. The way they think, speak, and live is markedly different from the rest of Catholics. When you speak to disengaged Catholics it becomes clear quickly that they don't get it, and more important, I think, it is alarmingly clear that they never did get it.

For years now we have been doing research in preparation to build major programs for each of these Catholic Moments: Baptism, First Reconciliation, First Communion, Confirmation, Marriage Preparation, and RCIA. One thing that amazed me as we threw ourselves into this work was that there is no moment in the catechetical development of a Catholic who was baptized as a child when we ask him or her to make a choice for Christ and his Church. At every step along the way we assume that people are committed to Christ and his Church—but in too many cases that is a false assumption, and it is hurting us enormously. Without a commitment of some kind, it is so much easier to walk away—and people are walking away at an alarming rate. But they are not waking up one day and saying, "I am not going to church anymore." For most people it is not a conscious decision. Most people just drift away from the Church. They may have been going to church every week until one Sunday their child had a soccer tournament and they missed Mass. Before you know it they are going three times a month or every second week. It continues in this way until they get completely out of the habit. But they come at Christmas because it just feels like the right thing to do. That's how we're losing them. It's not because they delved into Catholicism and discovered it has nothing to offer; it's not a well-informed and deliberate decision. They just drift away. This wouldn't be so rampant if our communities were stronger, because then we would notice they were drifting away and we would throw them a lifeline. The point is, they are gone, millions of them. But perhaps the more disturbing point is that when we had the chance we never really won them. We never helped them to form an effective relationship with Jesus and his Church. They never really got it. If they did, they would never have left.

What programs in your parish are designed to win people for God and his Church? Sure, everything we do is capable of having that effect. But what do you do as a parish that is specifically and intentionally designed to win people? We need to spend a lot of time and energy working out how we are going to win people if we are going to breathe new life into the Catholic Church today.

Once again, it all starts at the level of personal transformation. God wins us one at a time. Have you been won? Are you open to being won? Do you need to be won again? God wants to win you in new ways today. I hope God is using this book to win you in new ways. And I hope we will get serious about creating opportunities for God to win men, women, and children in our parishes.

BUILD

It was through the friendship of one man in particular that I experienced the build stage. Highly engaged Catholics have built a spiritual life. Many of them have done it over the course of decades by trial and error and incredible persistence. They did it this way because nobody showed them the way. I consider myself incredibly blessed to have been coached by someone who had already done the hard work.

It all started, as I have written before, when he encouraged me to stop by church for ten minutes each day on the way to school. It wasn't convenient, but this was a game changer for me. You can pray anywhere, but stop by your church for ten minutes each day for a week, and then tell me if it isn't different. This is where it all started for me. I know it sounds so basic—insignificant, almost. But game changers are usually simple.

After several weeks during which I spent ten minutes each day at church just talking to God, my spiritual coach suggested I start reading the Gospels for fifteen minutes a day also. It was here that I really met Jesus in a comprehensive way for the first time. The Gospels had been part of my life for as long as I could remember. All through Catholic school they were read or referenced, and every Sunday I would hear the Gospel read, but it never resonated with me. But now, finally, the Gospels penetrated my heart and Jesus came to life.

Little by little, brick by brick, my friend was helping me to build a spiritual life. He didn't thrust it all upon me at once. One at a time he introduced the key components of a vibrant spirituality. After several weeks of ingraining the habit of reading the Gospels, he suggested that I attend weekday Mass once each week. It was at daily Mass that I fell in love with the Mass . . . and I think it was through the daily Mass that I was won in a new way for the Church. I had been to Mass every Sunday of my life, but it was here in the daily Mass that it first really started to make sense. I have never been able to pinpoint exactly why that is, but there was something about the intimacy of that experience that allowed me to absorb it in a new way.

This friend was personally directing me in a process of continuous improvement.

Next, he suggested we spend a Saturday afternoon at a nursing home, visiting with those residents who rarely get visitors. Here

I was introduced to the Christian tradition of works of mercy, which naturally draw us out of ourselves. One of the biggest obstacles to spiritual development is getting caught up in ourselves. Works of mercy effortlessly liberate us from this obstacle.

A few weeks later he suggested that I go to Confession. I remember leaving that experience feeling elated, light as a feather, as if a great weight had been lifted from my back.

Throughout this entire process, week after week, I felt joy growing in my heart. I was happier, and in a very natural sense that was wonderful proof that I was on a new and important path.

Then one day we were driving home from playing basketball and he asked me if I would like to pray the rosary. I was embarrassed. My fourth- and fifth-grade teachers used to have us pray the rosary, but it had been years and I wasn't sure I remembered. He helped me through it, and by some grace I began praying the rosary each day. This simple, humble, and ancient prayer has been the source of incredible peace for me over the years. It never ceases to amaze me how this prayer slows me down and focuses me when I have the discipline to practice it.

From time to time, perhaps every three weeks or so, my friend would give me a spiritual book. By now I was devouring them. I was hungry to learn more. I felt like this great treasure had been before me my whole life, but I had essentially been ignoring it. I remember feeling angry that other people in my life had not helped me to discover it before now, and at the same time I felt grateful that I was experiencing it now.

But perhaps the most important aspect of my journey was one of the main points from chapter three. This one man helped me find answers to my questions. I had questions about prayer, I had questions about the Mass, I had questions about things I was reading in the Bible, questions about things I was reading in spiritual books, questions about things I would hear about Catholicism in the media. I had questions about life and he helped me discover answers to those questions.

I learned so much from him in this regard. He taught me that you don't have to have all the answers to help someone else grow in the faith; you just have to be willing to help him or her find the answers to the questions you cannot answer. He taught me that there are answers to the questions. In the process I came to one of my most strongly held convictions about our faith: People deserve answers to their questions.

At every step in the process I was being built up in knowledge and experience of God, and in every step I was being won in new and deeper ways.

You will notice that I mention *process* several times. It was a process. The man who was guiding me wasn't acting on a whim; he was intentionally sharing the faith with me and trying to lead me to a better life—the best life, in fact. He had spent decades developing a vibrant and practical spirituality for himself, and now he was freely sharing the wisdom of his experience. I was blessed to know him.

God wants to build in you a dynamic spirituality. He wants our parishes to help people of all ages build a spiritual life so that through our regular spiritual routines he can build and refine us in his image.

It is not enough for us to hope that this happens. We need process and intentionality. These are two of the key ingredients of effective evangelization. It isn't just going to happen. We need a plan.

SEND

The mistake here would be to focus on my public life as a speaker and writer. This work is certainly evangelization, but very few of us are called to evangelize in that way. We are, however, all called to evangelize. And the truth is, it is much easier to speak and write for large audiences than it is to take an interest in helping a few people whom God has placed in our lives to grow spiritually.

My first attempts at sharing the faith with others were clumsy and awkward. I was a teenager; my friends were interested in what teens are interested in. My best friends listened respectfully. My not-so-good friends dismissed my efforts out of hand. Most of all, I was impatient.

Over the years my approach to attracting people to Christ and his Church has become much more natural and patient. There are three keys to this approach: friendship, generosity, and answers.

Friendship is the most natural and effective way to share the faith with others. If we are friends and I say something that you disagree with, you are not likely to dismiss it without consideration. Out of the respect that is built through the course of a friendship, you will consider my point of view, even if you disagree with it. Inviting people to explore their questions of faith in a new way is asking them to rethink the way they live their lives—often in major ways. It is the respect that is born through friendship that allows people to let their guard down and consider a new way.

Christian friendship is not just about common interests; it is about helping each other become the-best-version-of-ourselves. A friendship that places the other person's best interests above our own selfish desires or agenda is quite rare in this world. Often when people first experience this kind of friendship they don't believe it. Christian friendship seems too good to be true in the current cultural landscape. And so it takes time to convince people that our friendship is genuine and rightly motivated. But it is this type of friendship that becomes the vehicle for the faith to spread.

The second key to Evangelization is generosity. Christianity, by its very nature, is generous. We are called to be generous with our time, talent, and treasure, but also with our love and compassion, going out of our way to generously serve those who cross our path. Generosity is disarming and attractive.

The third key, and in some ways the most important at this time in the life of the Church and culture, is helping people find answers to their questions. I cannot stress this point enough. We live in a time when more people have questions about Catholicism than ever before. Catholics have questions and non-Catholics have questions. One of the most effective ways to evangelize is to help people articulate their questions and help them to find answers to those questions. This form of evangelization becomes deeply personal, because it drives straight at the obstacles holding a person back from surrendering his or her life to God. Fulton Sheen wrote, "There are only one hundred people in the world who disagree with what the Church teaches. The rest disagree with what they think the Church teaches."

Ignorance is massive, and above most things I believe that people deserve answers to their questions. It is amazing how once we get a taste of the truth we develop an insatiable appetite for it. Once we catch a glimpse of the beauty of truth, the shallowness and emptiness of our culture is revealed.

We are all being called to share our faith with others. Through the beauty of Christian friendship, the goodness of outrageous generosity, and answering people's deepest questions, we are able to invite people to discover God, his Church, and the best way to live.

• • • • • • •

WIN. BUILD. SEND. This is the process of Evangelization. Too often when we talk about Evangelization in the Catholic Church we are asking people who have not been sufficiently won and built to go out into the world on a mission, and they are simply not ready. Most Catholics don't evangelize because they don't actually believe that Catholicism is a superior way of life. So why would they want to share it? They have not been won. Until we are won, we don't have the passion, that fire in our belly, to attract anyone else—and Christianity only genuinely grows through attraction.

Of late we have been talking about the New Evangelization. It is a theme that was first proposed by John Paul II and one that has been further emphasized by Benedict XVI. But here in the United States one has to question if there was an old evangelization. The Church in America has for the most part only ever grown by birth, marriage, and immigration. Though it is waning now, the luxury of a vibrant birth rate and large numbers of

Catholic immigrants allowed the Church to appear to be strong and growing. In truth, the Church in the United States has always grown, but not because we were committed to sharing the genius of Catholicism with others—and not because we are particularly good at it. The percentage of true converts who make up the growth of the Catholic Church in America is minuscule, especially if you take out those who converted in order to marry a Catholic.

The reason I share this is because if we are ever going to get really good at Evangelization, it is critical to recognize that we have never been particularly good at it.

The Win, Build, Send model works. And perhaps what it points out best is that we have been trying to accomplish this great mission of our Church—Evangelization—without a model. We need a model that is scalable and sustainable. There are no shortcuts. There is no point trying to send people if they have not been sufficiently won and built. This always ends in disaster. So when we talk about new efforts in the area of Evangelization it is impossible to have any real conversation without also considering what are we going to do to increase our success at winning and building people.

People don't fail because they want to fail. They fail because they don't know how to succeed. In terms of Evangelization, we have never really trained people how to do it, and much like we discovered in our discussion of the first sign, Prayer, if you just "see what happens," usually nothing does. We need a process for training Catholics to become really good at sharing the genius of Catholicism with others.

Everyone evangelizes about something, but most of us evangelize about the wrong things. Have you seen how passionate some people are when they talk about their iPhone? They tell you why they love it so much, point out the favorite apps and features, and by the time they are finished you probably want one yourself. That is evangelization. Other people evangelize about their car, their company, or their favorite vacation destination. It's amazing how animated we can become about things that are trivial. It is in our nature to evangelize. Sadly, many people have nothing better than their iPhone or favorite vacation place to evangelize about.

We are all evangelists. What are you evangelizing about?

Feeling Good About Being Catholic

Throughout the Win and Build stages, one of the things that happens to people is that they start to feel good about being Catholic. We don't talk anywhere near enough about this. In the context of a theological discussion or Church governance this might seem a little soft, but it is absolutely essential to the life and growth of the Church. Highly engaged Catholics feel good about being Catholic. They are inspired Catholics.

There are always reasons to feel down about our Catholic identity. Our own time is no different, and one of the costs of the sexual abuse scandal is that it has robbed many ordinary people of their ability to feel good about being Catholic. Tragically, while the media has attacked us relentlessly because of the sexual abuse scandals, we have not responded. We have not made our story known. We have allowed ourselves to be engulfed by negativity and failed to demonstrate our incredibly positive contributions.

In every place and time there is no shortage of reasons to feel really good about being Catholic. These include our social and spiritual contributions, the life we bring to communities, and the support we provide physically, emotionally, intellectually, and spiritually to literally hundreds of millions of people around the world every day. Our education and health care systems are just two examples. The list is endless but, sadly, little known. Ask Catholics to tell you three really great things about their Church and you quickly discover how little most people know about the role the Church plays in so many people's lives.

It is not that the good justifies the bad; rather, it is that the good is the result of authentically living the Catholic faith, while the bad reflects the fallibility of human beings. The bad usually says more about human nature than it does about the Catholic faith.

It is impossible to share the goodness and beauty of Christ and his Church with others if you don't feel good about being Catholic. So we'd better start spending some time thinking about this question: What will it take to get ordinary Catholics to feel good about being Catholic again?

The thing I have learned in all the years I have been speaking and writing is that people don't do anything until they are inspired. You can have all the right words on the page, but if people are not inspired, they won't respond to those words. Over the past twenty years there have been enormous efforts to make sure that we are teaching the truth of the Catholic faith in our faith formation programs, but in too many cases these programs are dry and uninspiring—so people don't respond. What were the disciples doing between the death of Jesus and Pentecost? Not much. What did they do after Pentecost? They changed the world. Seriously, these twelve guys literally changed the world. What happened? They got inspired. I realize that is not the theological jargon for what happened, but that's what happened. Catholics today need to be inspired. We need a massive outpouring (and inpouring) of the Holy Spirit.

People don't do anything until they are inspired, and once people are inspired there is almost nothing they can't do. Inspiring people is critical and something we have overlooked for too long.

Not surprisingly, the research discovered that Dynamic Catholics feel good about being Catholic. And they feel this way about Catholicism regardless of what is happening in their parish, regardless of the latest Church scandal, and regardless of how Catholicism has been distorted or abused throughout history. Catholicism is bigger than all this for them.

Again, let me stress, this is no small thing and not to be discounted.

One of the things I noticed very early on about the Dynamic Catholic Parish Book Program was that the excitement of passing out all those books to parishioners at Christmas and Easter just makes people feel good about being Catholic. I have noticed the same thing about different Catholic television ad campaigns. Often these advertisements are aimed at bringing people back to church, but I think we overlook or discount the tremendous value they have in inspiring those who do come to church every Sunday to feel good about being Catholic. From time to time you need to encourage those who are faithful, and it turns out that is one of the most effective ways to win back the disengaged.

How many Catholics are really proud to be Catholic? The truth is, morale is very low among Catholics today, and if we cannot change that, our ability to evangelize is going to be limited. You don't try to share something with others unless you feel really good about it yourself. And this might be the heart of the problem. The truth we are unwilling to face may just be that most Catholics don't feel good about being Catholic.

Beyond this overall feeling about being Catholic, the research surrounding the fourth sign of a Dynamic Catholic unveiled some interesting findings. First, even among highly engaged Catholics, Evangelization is the weakest link in the chain. When asked to rate themselves between 1 and 10 for each of the four signs, the 7% rated themselves at 6.8 or higher for Prayer, Study, and Generosity, but at just 4.9 for Evangelization.

When asked if they considered themselves evangelists, the overwhelming number of respondents said no. When asked to name an evangelist, more than 85 percent of highly engaged Catholics cited a non-Catholic evangelical Christian preacher. It is of significant interest to note that throughout the course of the interviews the most common person mentioned in any context was John Paul II. But when interviewees were asked who is an evangelist, John Paul II was not mentioned. This was particularly surprising to me, considering the fact that he preached the Gospel to more people than any other person in history.

So, even though Evangelization is a core behavior among highly engaged Catholics, they tend to do it in a more passive way than one might expect. One question they were asked was,

"What is the best Catholic book you have ever read?" After they responded they were then asked what they had done with the book after they had finished reading it. Invariably, they would say something like, "Oh, I gave that book to my friend Susie at work." They were asked a similar set of questions about the best Catholic CD they had ever heard. Again, with unerring consistency we heard answers such as, "I sent that to my son in California, who is struggling with . . ." In a very natural and nonthreatening way they were trying to share the faith with other people in their circle of influence by passing along books and CDs.

When Dynamic Catholics were asked what they did to try to share the faith with others, their top six answers were:

1. Pass books and CDs around.
2. Invite people to Catholic events.
3. Bring a godly perspective to conversations.
4. Learn the Catholic teachings on certain issues and be able to articulate them when the Church is attacked over those issues in social settings.
5. Help people discover answers to the questions that cause them to doubt the Catholic faith.
6. Demonstrate the love of God through faithful and generous friendship.

When asked about their first conscious attempts to share the faith with others, they all described the challenge of going beyond their comfort zone, and seemed to be in consensus that the first efforts were anxious and awkward attempts at evangelization.

Astoundingly, when asked if anyone had ever taught them how to evangelize, 99.4 percent of respondents said no.

But what was demonstrated over and over throughout the research is that the first and second signs (Prayer and Study) tend to give birth to the third and fourth signs (Generosity and Evangelization). The fourth sign cannot be increased in isolation. The first three signs make the fourth possible.

In summary, I think the research points out good and bad news in the area of Evangelization. The bad news is that as Catholics in America we are doing a very poor job of evangelizing the society we live in today. The good news is that we have never really tried. Most Catholics have never been taught how to evangelize in any systematic way, nor have they been convinced why they should do it.

The future of Evangelization depends upon our ability to win people for Christ and his Church, to build people in Christ and his Church, and to develop programs that teach people how to evangelize. Only then will we be able to send them out to change the world in any meaningful way.

Contagious Living

When it comes to Evangelization it seems that every Catholic's favorite quote is from Francis of Assisi: "Preach the Gospel at all times and when necessary, use words." There are two things to consider here. First, he did say to preach the Gospel at all times. Second, he didn't say never to use words. The quote is used too often as an excuse not to preach the Gospel, and especially not to actively evangelize.

Evangelization is to the Church what breathing is to a person.

If we stop doing it for long enough, we will die. The Church has been on life support in this area for decades now. And the truth is, it is our mission to evangelize. We exist to evangelize. It is our very existence. But we are neglecting it, and perhaps that is why our very existence in different places is being threatened. Isn't forgetting the reason for our existence the ultimate form of spiritual amnesia?

How do we start? We do so in the same way we are called to start with each of the four signs: with the smallest nonthreatening step. Incremental improvement can be applied to each of the four signs for incredible results.

The most fascinating thing about giving all the books away at Christmas and Easter was that inside the back of the book we placed an advertisement inviting people to visit DynamicCatholic.com if they liked the book and request six more copies at a very low cost. Every week we ship thousands of books in response to this simple ad. Some people might say, "That's great that you're selling a lot of books." Others might say, "That's fabulous that you're getting the message out to lots of people." But the real victory here is that we have given Catholics a simple way to evangelize. People don't buy six copies for themselves—they are passing them around to family and friends.

You see, if we are honest with each other, I think we can agree that most Catholics are not too comfortable or competent talking about their faith with others. But what the little experiment above proves is that most Catholics are comfortable giving someone a book. We have seen the same idea work with our CD program.

So, here is the action step: Try to do one thing each week to share the faith with someone who crosses your path. Perhaps you tell him you are going to pray for him and a situation he told you about. Perhaps you give her a book or CD. Perhaps you try to present God's perspective in a conversation. Or perhaps you invite someone to a Catholic event. Just do one thing each week. It could even be as simple as sharing a statistic or fact about Catholics with others: "Did you know that Catholic education saves the U.S. taxpayer eighteen billion dollars a year?" Or perhaps you sign up for a daily or weekly e-mail from a Catholic organization and forward it to a different friend depending on the content.

If every member of your parish did one thing each week to share the faith with others, how different would your parish be a year from now? If every Catholic in America did just one small act of evangelization each week, how would the Church grow over the next decade?

Little by little we can have an enormous impact. Just don't let what you can't do interfere with what you can do. Are you going to have to step outside your comfort zone? Yes, but you can do that a little bit at a time also.

If you place a bucket under a dripping tap, what happens? Drop by drop the bucket fills up, and then it overflows. The Win and the Build aspects of the Catholic journey are the drops of water; the Send stage is the overflow. If the bucket is sound and the tap is dripping, eventually it has to overflow. It has no choice.

When Catholicism is lived enthusiastically and generously it is incredibly attractive. In this way our lives become contagious.

When it comes to Evangelization, it seems to me that again we are plagued by the "let's see what happens" approach. We are paralyzed by inaction. Perhaps it is because we don't know what to do or how to do it, but if that is genuinely the problem, then let's get serious about solving it. Perhaps it is because enough of us have not yet been sufficiently won and built.

We started with the question, "If you could change the world, what would you change?" Here's the thing. We can change the world, and you can play a role in it. In fact, no group or organization is in a better position to change the world than Catholics.

CHAPTER SUMMARY

EVANGELIZATION

- The world is the way it is today because of human behavior. The world is constantly changing, for better or for worse. What makes it better or worse tomorrow? The way we live our lives today.

- Imagine all of the misery that could be avoided if we all just lived by the life-giving wisdom found in the Ten Commandments. Think for a moment on all the suffering that is caused because humanity has been unwilling to adopt a pattern of behavior and a social structure that celebrate the wisdom of the Ten.

- Every great civilization has concerned itself with this question: How is the best way to live? The rigor with which a person or culture approaches this question is very telling. It is of disturbing importance to note that the present culture has virtually no interest in pursuing this question. Today we are more interested in how we want to live than we are in discovering the best way to live.

- In our quest to discover the best way to live, we discover three universal principles:

  - The First Principle: You are here to become the-best-version-of-yourself.

  - The Second Principle: Virtue is the ultimate organizing principle, whether it is in a person's life, one's marriage, or the life of a nation.

  - The Third Principle: It is better to live with self-control than without it.

- Jesus's answer to how the best way to live was, "Love the Lord your God with all your heart, with all your soul, and with all your mind . . . and love your neighbor as yourself." (Matthew 26:37–39)

- God wants to *win* you with his love and wisdom; God wants to *build* you up spiritually so that you have the knowledge and habits to live in his love and walk in his ways; and God wants to *send* you out into the world to share his love with others. Win. Build. Send.

- There are three ways people are won: through truth, beauty, and goodness.

- Among the highly engaged Catholics who were interviewed as part of this research, 89 percent described a conversion experience—an event in their life that won them to a more engaged relationship with God.

- God wants to build in you a dynamic spirituality. He wants our parishes to help people of all ages build a spiritual life so that through our regular spiritual routines he can build and refine us in his image. It is not enough for us to hope that this happens. We need process and intentionality. These are two of the key ingredients of effective evangelization. It isn't just going to happen. We need a plan.

- Friendship is the most natural and effective way to share the faith with others.

- People don't fail because they want to fail. They fail because they don't know how to succeed.

- Throughout the Win and Build stages, one of the things that happens to people is that they start to feel good about being Catholic. We don't talk anywhere near enough about this. In the context of a theological discussion or Church governance this might seem a little soft, but it is absolutely essential to the life and growth of the Church. Highly engaged Catholics feel good about being Catholic. They are inspired Catholics.

- The research surrounding the fourth sign of a Dynamic Catholic unveiled some interesting findings. Even among highly engaged Catholics, Evangelization is the weakest link in the chain. When asked to rate themselves between 1 and 10 for each of the four signs, the 7% rated themselves at 6.8 or higher for Prayer, Study, and Generosity, but at just 4.9 for Evangelization.

- When Dynamic Catholics were asked what they did to try to share the faith with others, their top six answers were:

  1. Pass books and CDs around.
  2. Invite people to Catholic events.
  3. Bring a godly perspective to conversations.
  4. Learn the Catholic teachings on certain issues and be able to articulate them when the Church is attacked over those issues in social settings.
  5. Help people discover answers to the questions that cause them to doubt the Catholic faith.
  6. Demonstrate the love of God through faithful and generous friendship.

- Astoundingly, when asked if anyone had ever taught them how to evangelize, 99.4 percent of respondents said no.
- Evangelization is to the Church what breathing is to a person.
- Try to do one thing each week to share the faith with someone who crosses your path.
- The fourth sign of a Dynamic Catholic is Evangelization.

KEY CONCEPTS:

The Best Way to Live; Virtue; Self-Control; Evangelization; Win, Build, Send.

Chapter Six

A NEW LEVEL OF THINKING

"**IF YOU ARE WHAT YOU SHOULD BE** you will set the world ablaze." These words were famously penned in the fourteenth century by Catherine of Siena. It's an arresting idea for a number of reasons. We all have a sense of who we are capable of being, and a sense that we are not quite living up to our potential. But the quote also rightly points out that there are natural consequences for the whole world when we find and live out our mission in life. When we are faithful to who God created us to be, and what God calls us to do, incredible things happen. The opposite of the quote is also true: If you are *not* what you should be, you will *not* set the world ablaze.

Today, we need to consider this idea from three perspectives: as individuals, as a parish, and as a Church. Are we what we should be as individuals? Is your parish the-best-version-of-itself? As a Church, are we being faithful to who God created us to be, and what God is calling us to do? If we give these questions any real thought, I believe we come to the conclusion that on all three levels—as individuals, as a parish, and as a Church—we are not quite who we should be. This conclusion is reached because the evidence suggests that we are not setting the world ablaze.

During the early days of the civil rights movement James Weldon Johnson wrote, "We need to hold a mirror up to this country." In the same way, I believe we need to hold a mirror up to our lives, parishes, and Church. We cannot be who we should be or do what we are called to do if we do not have regular moments of honest self-examination. We need to see ourselves in the mirror—the beauty and the warts. The way forward to a vibrant and relevant future requires a rigorous honesty about our strengths and weaknesses, and a willingness to change and grow.

The starting point of a rigorous self-examination is an assessment of where we are today.

I have dedicated much of my adult life to encouraging people to embrace the genius of Catholicism, and I intend to continue to do so. Some days I am sure I am making a difference, but on other days I get terribly discouraged. You see, in the quiet moments when I am alone with my thoughts, I am deeply troubled about the state of the Church.

The tide on Catholicism is going out. More than thirty million Americans now consider themselves former Catholics. That's ten percent of the U.S. population, more than the entire population of twenty of the fifty states, or more than the entire population of Canada. Former Catholic is now the second-largest religious affiliation in this country, after Catholic. Young adults are abandoning the Church at an alarming rate. Of those who remain, the largest challenges are disengagement and the indifference it breeds.

More than 70 percent of American Catholics don't attend church on Sunday. Only 17 percent attend every Sunday. Engagement among those who do come to church is marginal at best. Young people in particular are leaving the Church at a frightening pace and they are not returning later in life. Among young adults between the ages of twenty and thirty, less than 15 percent attend Mass on any given Sunday. We have told ourselves they will come back when they get married or have children, but they are not coming back. The number of Catholic weddings each year in America has decreased by sixty thousand over the past four decades, even though the number of Catholics has increased by more than sixteen million during the same period. We have closed more than three thousand parishes in the past twenty years. We have closed a Catholic school in the United States every four days for twenty years. Vocations are rising but are still insufficient. Ten short years from now, as many as fifty percent of American parishes will not have a resident priest. Many parishes and whole dioceses are in serious financial trouble. We are failing to speak to the real issues of people's lives. The average Catholic has an elementary understanding of the faith. Many Catholics are ashamed to be Catholic. All of these issues are interrelated.

Any other organization would be alarmed, and yet "business as usual" seems to be our attitude. When was the last time you saw a McDonald's restaurant close? How would the company respond if it had to close three thousand of its locations?

More disturbing still is that much of our planning on both a national and a diocesan level is focused on dealing with the challenges of a shrinking Church in the coming decades. The idea that this exodus will continue seems to have been accepted by much of our leadership as if there is nothing we can do about it, as if it is a fait accompli. Are you okay with that? I am not. I would like to see something done to stem and then turn the tide. Besides, isn't the idea of a smaller Church in direct conflict with our mission?

If you are wondering what will happen if we continue on our present course, just look across the Atlantic Ocean. In Europe the situation is even worse, and here we find a prophecy of what we can expect if we do not respond differently than they did to the signs we are now discussing. Christianity in Europe, and Catholicism in particular, is being marginalized by secularism and socialism at an ever-increasing pace. Church attendance in many countries is half of what we are describing as a crisis in America today. Germany has 12 percent Sunday Mass attendance, Italy has 11 percent, France 4 percent, and the Scandinavian countries around 1 percent. In Ireland the Catholic Church is imploding. England is among the bright lights of the Catholic world in Western Europe at this time: Catholicism is once again the dominant religion of the land for the first time since Henry VIII and the Reformation, which propelled the splintering of Christianity. In my own homeland, Australia, secularism is taking its toll on Catholics in the same way it has in most advanced nations. Too many people seem bored, fed up, and disinterested with all things spiritual, particularly organized religion and especially the

Catholic Church. There is a Chinese proverb that says, "If we don't change our direction, we are likely to end up where we are headed." It is time to consider this.

The Way Forward

What's the problem? To put it in its simplest terms, what we are doing is not working. Tens of millions of American Catholics have left the Church, millions more are leaving each year, and among those who remain the level of disengagement is staggeringly high.

Research conducted by the Dynamic Catholic Institute and other organizations suggests that the reason for this problem is that the Catholic Church in America is failing to meet people where they are and speak meaningfully about the real issues of concern in their lives. What are those issues? What is it that the people of our times are grappling to understand? For what circumstances are they hungry for practical solutions? Money issues, marriage problems, addiction, the challenge of raising children, unemployment, jobs that are unfulfilling, a yearning to grow spiritually, problems with their manager or colleagues at work—these are the everyday issues that people are dealing with, and the Gospel speaks to all of them in one way or another. Yet we seem unable to establish the connection between the Gospel and the everyday lives of those who fill the pews. Is it not obvious that we are failing to speak meaningfully about the very real issues of people's lives? We need to make the connection between the life and teachings of Jesus Christ and the stuff of real life in the twenty-first century.

I often ask my audiences what the largest Catholic church is in their city. Someone usually says, "Saint Mary's" or "Saint Paul's" or "the cathedral." Then I ask them, "Is that because it is the biggest church or because the most people attend church there on a Sunday?" They usually say it is because this parish or that has the most registered parishioners.

I then explain that they are probably wrong, and that Saint Mary's or Saint Paul's or the cathedral is most likely not the largest Catholic church in their area. There is probably a nondenominational church that more Catholics attend every Sunday than the church they identified. More than 50 percent of the population of these churches are former Catholics, and many of the churches are enormous. Millions of former Catholics flock to these places every Sunday.

Why do people go there? The better question is, why are people flocking there with unbridled enthusiasm? If you think it is about the coffee and the stadium seating, you are sorely mistaken. It's because they feel welcome, they experience a sense of community, the message speaks to the real issues of their lives, and they are continually directed in practical ways to grow spiritually.

Our non-Catholic Christian brothers and sisters are far superior at meeting people where they are and speaking to the real issues of their lives, and while they remain so they will continue to win millions of Catholics away from our pews and into their megachurches every year.

While none of this is particularly a secret, our response has been to ignore their success at speaking to the real issues of people's lives and helping ordinary people to grow spiritually. I cannot tell you how many times I hear Catholic teachers and leaders scoff at their approach, as if our approach is superior even though it is failing.

Let's face it, we have known for decades that the average Catholic judges his or her experience of Mass by the quality of the music and the homily. So why haven't we mastered both of these? Would we be compromising ourselves in any way if people came away from church on Sunday truly inspired by the music and the homily? Given that we have known that these are the two things that tend to engage disengaged Catholics in the Mass, why hasn't there been a focused initiative to improve the quality of both? I realize these are not the most important aspects of the Mass, but they are clearly a bridge or an obstacle for most people.

Looking down on the disengaged or criticizing them for not being more engaged doesn't cause them to become engaged.

Along these lines, one disturbing trend that I have noticed is that there is more and more talk about the Church and less and less talk about God among those directing the Church at every level today (both lay and clerical). It seems often forgotten that people do not exist for the Church, but rather, the Church exists for the people. Is our priority to preserve the institution or to serve the people the institution exists to serve? Is God more concerned with his people or with the institution of the Church?

Do you know anyone who thinks all is well for the Catholic Church in America? Does anyone think the Church is headed unquestionably in a great direction? I don't. So surely we can all agree that our current response to the problems we face as a Church has been woefully inadequate.

Is the Catholic Church the-best-version-of-itself? And of all the things in this world shouldn't we work to make it so, or at least nudge it in that direction? Is the Church a beacon of excellence in the world?

I don't know anyone who would say that the Catholic Church is executing its mission in the world today with great effectiveness and efficiency. There are, of course, pockets of excellence and success. Part of a new level of thinking should be more effective systems and processes for identifying and sharing these best practices far and wide.

Sharing best practices requires a level of collaboration that is underdeveloped in the Catholic Church, to say the least. Our provincial model does not lend itself naturally to this. One of the reasons we are spending so much time and resource on building world-class programs for the Catholic Moments (Baptism, First Reconciliation, First Communion, Confirmation, Marriage Preparation, RCIA, Lent, and Advent) at The Dynamic Catholic Institute is because the resources available for these are failing to engage people.

One of the first questions we floated as our team began work on these programs was: Why have world-class programs not been developed in each of these areas? One million Catholics in the United States experience Confirmation each year, for example. Clearly there is a need for a top-notch program that is highly engaging. So why don't we have one? We can learn a great deal from the answer. Too often we are more concerned with *our* practices than we are with *best* practices. We take the Frank Sinatra approach and do it "my way." As a result, there are fifteen thousand parishes in the United States today and fifteen thousand different confirmation programs. Many of them may be good, some of them may have moments of real genius, and all of them are developed by very well-intentioned people, but not a single one is truly world-class.

Here is the key insight that convinced me to launch into the enormous task of developing programs for each of the Catholic Moments: No parish in America has enough talent or money to develop the best programs in the world. If we want to do these things right we need to get together and collaborate to make it happen. We need to seek out the best aspects of everything that is available today, and bring the best Catholic minds of our time together, if we are to produce something truly extraordinary. And, in my personal opinion, we need to find a way to make these resources available to parishes for free or at very little cost once they are developed. There is no point having world-class programs if half the parishes cannot afford to purchase them.

We need to develop a hunger for best practices.

It is essential to the future of Catholicism that we come to the realization that the thinking that got us here will probably not transform the Church in our time into a dynamic and relevant institution. If the Church is to become vibrant again it is of vital importance that we begin thinking on a whole new level. Albert Einstein observed, "The significant problems we face cannot be solved with the same level of thinking we were at when we created them."

When I say this I am not talking about throwing away doctrines and dogmas, or even overturning traditions. I realize such words can easily be construed as such. But rather, I am suggesting that we can operate and communicate much more effectively if we start thinking on a new level.

We Need a Game-Changer

What would it take to make your parish the church in town that everyone is curious about? What would it take to make your church the one in your area that everyone has to come to at least once just to check it out? Those planning to open a megachurch spend weeks and months thinking about questions like these. They study the area and the demographics, and they target particular groups—and Catholics are always one of the groups they target. It might be the right question, and it might not. But I think it demonstrates that they are thinking on a completely different level than we are. We need a new level of thinking.

The first step toward this new level of thinking is to stop playing defense. I love sports. What sports? Any sports. I love watching and I love playing. There is something about sports that captures the essence of life, the struggle that is life, and the quest of the human spirit. I also love Catholicism, though I am deeply troubled by our current approach. One thing that occurs to me is that I don't know of any sport that you can win by just playing defense, and the Catholic Church has been playing defense for an awfully long time. Most coaches will tell you that the best form of defense is a good offense. But we have been playing defense for decades, for longer than I have been alive. Christianity is by its very nature proactive. Our current passive and defensive posture is not Christian. It's time for us to get out of maintenance mode and refocus on our mission. It's time to start playing a little offense. We need a new level of thinking. The old thinking is defensive thinking.

Throughout this book we have explored a number of key concepts: continuous improvement; incremental spirituality; continuous learning; best practices; game changers; personal transformation; "I can do that!"; intentionality; engagement and disengagement; meeting people where they are; Win, Build, Send; you get what you measure; the 80/20 principle; and the four signs model, to name just a few. These key concepts represent a new level of thinking. They are largely missing from our current approach, and that needs to change. Start thinking about how well you apply these key concepts in your life. Every time you get involved in your parish in any way, try to apply one of these key concepts.

I have spent the past twenty years traveling the world. I have visited and served Catholic parishes in more than fifty countries, and in the United States I have visited more than two thousand parishes. Inspiring people to discover the genius of Catholicism is one of my passions. Eighty-five percent of my time is spent pursuing this passion. But for four days each month I enter into a very different realm: the world of corporate America. On these days I work with some of the most admired companies in the world. I spend 15 percent of my time making a living as a business consultant. My job: to help a company's people attain peak performance personally and professionally, and to find game changers for their business.

What is a game changer? It is an idea, a strategy, a product or service, a process or person that can create a breakthrough and take an organization to the next level.

Michael Jordan was a game changer for the Chicago Bulls. The iPod did it for Apple. The Pixar digital animation process did it for Disney. Tiger Woods was a game changer for golf. Lean manufacturing did it for the American auto industry. The idea that flying could be fun did it for Southwest Airlines. Breakfast did it for McDonald's. Cell phones and the Internet were game changers for the whole world.

The thing about game changers is that in hindsight they can seem ridiculously obvious and simple. When most people go looking for a game changer they usually spend their time and energy looking for that enormous idea that will change everything. But the reality is most game changers are small and simple. It is the simplicity of a game changer that makes implementation and broad adoption possible.

The Catholic Church in America needs a game changer. This implicitly means that most Catholics also need a game changer for their individual spirituality. I hope the four signs will be that game changer.

The Four Signs

The research shows that if you help Catholics develop habits in each of the four signs with focused and specific outcomes in mind, they become among the most highly engaged Catholics.

Imagine what could happen if from our first contact with Catholics as children we ingrained the four signs as lifelong habits. Imagine if we built all our catechetical and educational programs to nurture and develop the four signs. Imagine if your priest or deacon made a connection in his homily every Sunday between the Gospel and one of the four signs. Imagine the intentionality we could drive.

I asked one priest to print the four signs in his bulletin each week. Then I asked him each Sunday at the beginning of his homily to say, "Today's Gospel is about the third sign!" or "What Jesus is speaking to us about in the Gospel today is the first sign." It was just one line at the beginning of every homily, but it drove intentionality, and it was amazing to see how his people responded.

This I know for sure: Only a few small groups of people make the effort to develop a daily routine of prayer if they are not taught how to do so. Even fewer develop the habit of continuous learning and study unless they are guided in practical ways. People don't become champions of generosity without some coaching around the topic. And the chances of someone becoming passionate about and effective at evangelization without some training in this area are almost zero. These things do not happen on their own; they require real intentionality. The four signs provide the context for that intentionality, which could be the game changer we are looking for.

Imagine if a parish approached the four signs with a four-year plan. For the first year it focuses on helping everyone in the parish develop a daily routine of prayer. In year two, the parish focuses on helping its members become continuous learners. The third year is dedicated to learning about the role of generosity in our lives and becoming more generous, as a parish and as individuals. In the fourth year we implement a system of evangelization.

Just helping everyone in the parish develop a daily routine of prayer would be a complete game changer for any parish.

Now take it a step further. Imagine if a whole diocese committed to a four-year plan to raise up its people in the four signs.

But maybe I am wrong. Perhaps the four signs are not the game changer. I am open to that. But if that is the case, let's get busy looking for the game changer that the Catholic Church in America needs so desperately today. Goethe wrote, "Be bold and mighty forces will come to your aid." It is this boldness that the Catholic Church needs at every level today. The mighty forces that will come to our aid are Father, Son, and Holy Spirit. They are appalled by our timidity, which is the mark of a lukewarm worldling. "Be Bold, Be Catholic." This is our motto at Dynamic Catholic. And if we can muster the courage for this boldness, something wonderful will happen. What will then emerge from this boldness? A Catholic vision for our time.

Unless a great Catholic vision emerges for our time, the slow demise will continue. Proverbs 29:18 states this clearly: "Where there is no vision, the people will perish."

Gandhi had a vision for India, a dream for his homeland.

It was simply this: "A free and independent India." Over and over again he repeated his vision in his writings and speeches, in casual conversation and in media interviews. During his time if you had asked Indians, "What is Gandhi's dream?" they would have told you, "A free and independent India." You would not have gotten dozens or hundreds of different answers. You would have gotten just one. Gandhi was an incredibly effective communicator. He may have been the unintentional father of modern branding, because the way he used this simple phrase over and over again is exactly the way multinational corporations ingrain their brands in our hearts and minds today. My point is, if you asked everyone in your parish to explain the mission of your parish, how many different answers do you think you would get? If you asked all seventy-seven million Catholics in America today to briefly describe the mission of the Catholic Church, how many different answers do you think you would get?

For a mission-driven people, our mission is frightfully undefined in the modern world. It is impossible to separate this discovery from the fact that we are just drifting organizationally.

There have been very dynamic moments in our past, but in each case they were times of focus and rigorous intentionality. When has the Church been most dynamic?

A strong case can be made for the dynamic nature of the first three hundred years of Christianity, all of which was built primarily on the development of small groups, which encouraged people to share their lives.

The great influx of new Christians entering the Church during Constantine's reign in the 300s could certainly be called dynamic. It also led to the rise of monasticism.

In the early Middle Ages, the development and rapid growth of monastic communities certainly showed a dynamic process of Church growth. Through their vows of stability, preserving the scholarship of the ancient world, establishing islands of peace in a chaotic world, being dynamos of prayer, they became the foundation of Western civilization. The basic values we live and teach today were preserved and transmitted by the monastic communities.

The High Middle Ages, especially the 1200s, are seen by many historians as the pinnacle of Western Christianity. The rise of the Gothic cathedrals, which only happened with the dynamic collaboration between the clergy and laity in the medieval cities; the Franciscans; the Dominicans; the rise of the universities; and the writings of Aquinas and Bonaventure all emerged during this period. We still live off their legacy.

The Counter-Reformation was quite dynamic, with the institutional changes challenging the status quo, the influence of the Carmelite reforms of Teresa of Avila and John of the Cross, Ignatius and the Jesuits, the developments in the devotional life of the Church, the confraternities of prayer and Christian doctrine, and the missions of the Franciscans and Jesuits in the Americas and Asia.

While the Church suffered in Europe in the nineteenth and twentieth centuries, it was also a period of great missionary expansion in Africa and Asia. And important for the United States during this period were the expansion of the American Church, the councils of Baltimore, the establishment of the Catholic school system, lay confraternities, expansion of Catholic colleges across the

United States, and the growth of religious communities of women.

But in terms of what must be the most dynamic period of the Church, it has to be the years between 33 and about 150, the experience of the Apostolic Church, which through the New Testament and Tradition has given to us the experience of faith in the risen Jesus Christ. It is in the New Testament that we have the core paradigm of what our Christian vocation means. When we move away from Scripture, we alienate ourselves from our heart, since we can only find our true heart in the heart of Jesus.

It is time for another great and dynamic period in Catholic history.

The World Has Changed

But the world has changed dramatically since even the most recent of these dynamic periods in Catholic history. The image of Catholicism has suffered massively. The Catholic brand is deteriorating. I appreciate that some may be offended by my referring to a Catholic brand, but whether we choose to accept it or not, we do have a brand, and it is in trouble.

People have lost confidence in our brand. It seems every time we do or say anything, we alienate or enrage a group of people—often large groups of people. I realize this is necessary if we are to proclaim the truth in the world, but isn't it possible for us also to do things that the whole world can cheer?

Perhaps it's time we did some great service to humanity again. I know, we do a great service to humanity every day. But perhaps it is time for something bigger, something bolder. There is so much we could do. There is very little we could not do if we boldly got behind a vision.

Humor me by considering just one example. I don't hold it up as the ultimate example; just as an example. If over the next decade the Catholic Church decided to end child poverty in America, we could do it. It's just one idea, and maybe it's not the right one. But here's the thing: Who is going to criticize the Church for trying to end poverty among children in America?

If we are to move forward in a modern world dominated by every type of media, image is important. It is more important than ever before. More than most people, I wish it was not, but wishing will not make it so. At the moment, the media is dictating our image. As a result, if you ask people what comes to mind when they think of the Catholic Church, the answers you get primarily surround sexual abuse and the Church's position on homosexuality.

We need to do something big and bold, something that everyone can agree is a good thing, whether they are Catholic or not. We need to change the conversation if we are going to engage the people of our times.

John F. Kennedy stood up and announced that by the end of the sixties we would land a man on the moon. In doing so he captured the imagination of the whole nation, and spurred innovation in a thousand ways. That's what bold initiative does.

If together Catholics announced that we are going to put an end to child poverty in America by the end of the decade, it would energize people and mobilize them.

People follow bold missions. They want to give their lives to something bigger than themselves. We should be able to present them with a vision that inspires them to throw themselves into it with reckless abandon.

The Catholic Church in America is waiting to be reinvigorated. The whole world needs to be reintroduced to the love and wisdom of Jesus Christ. These two realities are connected.

I believe that God is at work in the world, in our lives, and in the Church. I have seen plenty of evidence to support this in my own life. I have felt the hand of God on my shoulder and heard him whisper in my ear, directing me whenever I was open to his truth. And yet, I must admit that I am baffled when I wonder what God is doing in his Church today. This state of bafflement leads me to remind myself that God has always worked in cooperation with humanity, and this puts me in that uncomfortable place of questioning how well we are cooperating with God at all levels of the Church today.

It is disturbingly clear that our present efforts are focused more on surviving than on thriving, on containment than on expansion, on the institution rather than the people the institution exists to serve. And a little tweak here and there is not going to turn the tide. In fact, our current approach is failing even to stem the tide. Are we brave enough to rethink our direction? I don't know. What I do know is that the possibilities are incredible. Catholicism is a sleeping giant. With more than 1.2 billion Catholics worldwide and almost eighty million Catholics in the United States alone, imagine what we could accomplish if we could awaken the sleeping giant, inspire a bigger future, and align together behind a bold plan.

It was the search for a game changer that led to the research upon which this book is based. I hope you have found the ideas in these pages helpful. I hope they have inspired you and disturbed you. I hope they have comforted you in your afflictions and afflicted you in your comfort. I hope these words have given you reason to feel really good about being Catholic again. Most of all, I hope they fill you with hope. Yes, we have big problems, but they are insurmountable only if we refuse to face them. They are insurmountable only if we refuse to gather the best minds of our times and invite them to solve our problems with us. They are insurmountable only if we separate them and ourselves from Jesus, who remains the way, the truth, and the life.

How Will You Respond?

This is the real question. Is this just another book, or is this a moment in your life when you will decide to step it up a notch, get more involved, and be the difference that makes the difference?

Are you ready to let Jesus take you to the next level in your spiritual life? When enough people answer yes to this question, the Church will again become fresh and vibrant, relevant and invigorated. Real hope for the future comes from giving everything to the present. If we give ourselves generously to the present God will transform us, and in turn he will use us not only to transform our parishes and the Church, but to change the world.

In a land where there are no musicians; in a land where there are no storytellers, teachers, and poets; in a land where there are no men and women of vision and leadership; in a land where there are no legends, saints, and champions; in a land where there are no dreamers, the people will most certainly perish. But you and I, we are the music makers; we are the storytellers, teachers, and poets; we are the men and women of vision and leadership; we are the legends, the saints, and the champions; and we are the dreamers of the dreams. Let us sit with God for a few minutes each day and dream with him, and with the vision he places in our hearts, go out into the world with a contagious love that cannot be ignored.

Be bold. Be Catholic. When the Catholic faith is actually lived it is incredibly potent.

CHAPTER SUMMARY

A NEW LEVEL OF THINKING

- "If you are what you should be you will set the world ablaze." —Catherine of Siena
- The way forward to a vibrant and relevant future requires a rigorous honesty about our strengths and weaknesses, and a willingness to change and grow. The starting point of a rigorous self-examination is an assessment of where we are today.
- The tide is going out on Catholicism in America, and business as usual is not going to turn the tide.
- What would it take to make your parish the church in town that everyone is curious about? What would it take to make your church the one in your area that everyone has to come to at least once just to check it out? Those planning to open a megachurch spend weeks and months thinking about questions like these. They study the area and the demographics, and they target particular groups—and Catholics are always one of the groups they target. It might be the right question, and it might not. But I think it demonstrates that they are thinking on a completely different level than we are. We need a new level of thinking.
- Unless a great Catholic vision emerges for our time, the slow demise will continue. Proverbs 29:18 states clearly, "Where there is no vision, the people will perish."
- Throughout this book we have explored a number of key concepts: continuous improvement; incremental spirituality; continuous learning; best practices; game changers; personal transformation; "I can do that!"; intentionality; engagement and disengagement; meeting people where they are; Win, Build, Send; you get what you measure; the 80/20 principle; and the

four signs model, to name just a few. These key concepts represent a new level of thinking. They are largely missing from our current approach, and that needs to change. Start thinking about how well you apply these key concepts in your life. Every time you get involved in your parish in any way, try to apply one of the concepts.

- The Catholic Church in America needs a game changer. This implicitly means that most Catholics also need a game changer for their individual spirituality.
- Imagine what would happen if we intentionally organized everything we do in the Church around the four signs. Imagine if from cradle to grave we focused on helping Catholics develop the four signs.
- Are you ready to let Jesus take you to the next level in your spiritual life? When enough people answer yes to this question, the Church will again become fresh and vibrant, relevant and invigorated. Real hope for the future comes from giving everything to the present. If we give ourselves generously to the present God will transform us, and in turn he will use us not only to transform our parishes and the Church, but to change the world.

KEY CONCEPTS:

Best Practices; Contagious Living; Vision: Game-Changers; Self-Examination.

Epilogue

EVERYTHING IS TRIGGERED BY SOMETHING.

What triggers engagement? What happened to spark a deeper level of interest and commitment among the 7%? Were they born Dynamic Catholics? Are they God's favorites?

I have purposely saved one of the most interesting facts gathered from the research to close this book with, because I think it provides a great starting point for parishes.

In Chapter Five I wrote:

> *Among the highly engaged Catholics who were interviewed as part of this research, 89 percent described a conversion experience—an event in their life that won them to a more engaged relationship with God. Some of them used this language and described it as a conversion, but many of them described it with other language. Some simply said things such as, "That was when I really got it for the first time!" Some "got it" by going on a retreat, on a pilgrimage, or to a conference, others got it by reading a book or listening to a CD, and still others got it when they experienced a life-altering event or the death of a loved one.*

Something happens in the life of a Dynamic Catholic to trigger engagement. They are not born highly engaged. They are not God's favorites. Something triggers a new level of engagement.

I hope this book will be a trigger for many. But the research revealed that in most parishes there was one trigger that was accounting for the overwhelming number of Dynamic Catholics. In some parishes it was a weekend experience such as Christ Renews His Parish (CRHP) or Cursillo, and in other parishes it was small faith groups or mission trips. But in the overwhelming majority of parishes, one thing was the trigger for more than half of the 7%. What is it in your parish?

Chances are, something is already working in your parish to effectively increase engagement among your people. Find out what it is and celebrate it. For example, if you have a parish with one thousand members, the research suggests that seventy people (7 percent) are driving everything in your parish. Find out who those seventy people are and what triggered their engagement. In one parish we discovered that fifty-three of the seventy had been through CRHP. The pastor of that parish asked me how that information should change the way they do things. This is what I told him:

> "You have discovered what is working. Now use that knowledge to create great intentionality in your parish. Allow that information to create a bold mandate for your parish—"In the next three years we would like every person in the parish to attend a CRHP retreat!" Then measure it, publish the results, thank

> people for responding, and celebrate your progress. Make buttons that say, "I DID IT!" Market it extensively in the parish. Mention it every chance you get in formal parish communications, teach people who have already done it to mention it often in casual conversation, and invite people personally to attend. If you know this one program is most effective in your parish, champion it. If it works, focus on it. Intentionally place the most effective trigger at the center of your parish's life."

I am looking forward to seeing what happens in that parish.

One thing to keep in mind is that the trigger may not be the most important thing theologically, but it is the bridge that carries people from where they are to where God is calling them to be. It is the bridge that carries them to the most important things.

Most of all, remember that people need to be invited—so invite them. They often need to be invited many times before they will respond. Don't be timid about it. You are inviting them to a much better life. It is amazing how many people just need to be invited to go deeper and given a simple format that helps them to do it. Invitation remains one of the most effective tools for spreading Christianity.

And regardless of where people are in the journey, encourage them. A reporter asked me a few weeks ago, "What are you trying to accomplish?"

"I am just trying to encourage people to take one step closer to God each day!" was my reply.

For all these years that I have been speaking and writing, I have been trying to figure out the best way to reach people. At the end of the day, it really is quite simple: People need to be encouraged. The young couple wrestling with their children two pews in front of you at Mass—they need to be encouraged. The priest, young or old, trying to lead your community—he needs to be encouraged. The young man and woman looking around wondering why they are the only ones their age in church—they need to be encouraged. Everyone needs to be encouraged. To be encouraged is one of humanity's great needs and one of the greatest works of the Holy Spirit.

Heisman trophy winner Danny Wuerffel tells the story of a voice he heard throughout his whole life. He heard it in first grade when he was trying to win a race. "You're the fastest boy in the grade, Danny!" the voice said. He won. He heard it in third grade as he turned his head to look at a classmate's paper and cheat on a test. "You're a good boy, Danny. Don't cheat." He didn't. He said he heard that voice spurring him on and guiding him all throughout his time as a world-class athlete and competitor.

Flash forward to the birth of Danny's first son. Danny's mother was in town helping with the baby for a couple of weeks. One day Danny walked past the nursery, where she was rocking the newborn. "You're so strong, Jonah," she said. "You're such a good boy." Danny paused. Her words sounded so familiar.

Later that same day Danny walked by the nursery again. His mother was still talking to the baby. "You're so smart, Jonah. What a wonderful boy you are." Danny Wuerffel broke into tears. The voice he had heard his whole life was the voice of his mother and father. It was the voice of love and encouragement.

There is no substitute for encouragement. I hope this book has encouraged you. I hope the great encourager—the Holy Spirit—inspires you to become a great encourager of others. I hope our parishes will become communities of encouragement, so that together we can re-propose the genius of Catholicism to the people of our times.

ABOUT THE AUTHOR

Matthew Kelly has dedicated his life to helping people and organizations become the-best-version-of-themselves. Born in Sydney, Australia, he began speaking and writing in his late teens while he was attending business school. Since that time, four million people have attended his seminars and presentations in more than fifty countries.

Today Kelly is an internationally acclaimed speaker, author, and business consultant. His books have been published in more than twenty-five languages, have appeared on the *New York Times*, *Wall Street Journal*, and *USA Today* bestseller lists, and have sold more than fifteen million copies.

He is also the founder of the Dynamic Catholic Institute, a Cincinnati-based nonprofit organization whose mission is to reenergize the Catholic Church in America by developing world-class resources that inspire people to rediscover the genius of Catholicism.

Kelly is also president at Floyd Consulting, a Florida-based management consulting firm.

His personal interests include golf, piano, literature, spirituality, and spending time with his wife, Meggie, and their children, Walter, Isabel, Harry, Ralph, and Simon.

NOTES

NOTES

NOTES

THE
DYNAMIC CATHOLIC
INSTITUTE

[MISSION]

To re-energize the Catholic Church in America by developing world-class resources that inspire people to rediscover the genius of Catholicism.

[VISION]

To be the innovative leader in the New Evangelization helping Catholics and their parishes become the-best-version-of-themselves.

DynamicCatholic.com
Be Bold. Be Catholic.®

The Dynamic Catholic Institute
5081 Olympic Blvd
Erlanger, Kentucky 41018
Phone: 859-980-7900
Email: info@DynamicCatholic.com